Toddle On Over

Developing Infant & Toddler Literature Programs

Robin Works Davis

Alleyside Press ®

Fort Atkinson, Wisconsin

Ch

Published by Alleyside Press,
an imprint of Highsmith Press LLC
Highsmith Press
W5527 Highway 106
P.O. Box 800
Fort Atkinson, Wisconsin 53538-0800
1-800-558-2110

© Robin Works Davis, 1998
Cover design: Frank Neu

The paper used in this publication meets the minimum requirements of American National Standard for Information Science — Permanence of Paper for Printed Library Material. ANSI/NISO Z39.48-1992.

Library of Congress Cataloging-in-Publication Data

Davis, Robin Works, 1962–
    Toddle on over : developing infant & toddler literature programs / Robin Works Davis.
        p. cm.
    Includes bibliographical references and index.
    ISBN 1-57950-000-5 (softcover : alk. paper)
    1. Children's libraries--Activity programs--United States.
    2. Libraries--Services to toddlers--United States. I. Title.
Z718. 2. U6D38 1998
027.62 ' 5--dc21   97-42216
                                                    CIP

Contents

Preface

Working with infants and toddlers is not only one of the most rewarding professional experiences an adult can have, it is also an energizing, forever enlivening activity! My reward, in over nine years experience sharing literature with this age group, has been the many parents and children who learned to love books and reading through our programs.

The spur for all librarians and teachers who are interested in growing new readers is an expanding body of evidence that these early programs really do make a difference for children. Researchers continue to discover important information about babies that can be directly related to infant/toddler programs. Those scholars who once thought that children entered into the world as blank slates now know that infants have very sophisticated brains. Research is also showing that in the earliest months of life, a staggering amount of brain development occurs. Children's intelligence—actual brain growth—and well being are directly affected by their environment, including nourishment, intellectual challenges, and adequate affection. What this means is that babies exposed to an environment with more stimulation will develop more synapses (brain cell connections) than those who are not stimulated. Or more simply, that the talking, holding, singing, playing and exploring we do with a baby adds up to an increased capacity for learning that lasts throughout that child's life.

If you would, imagine for a moment being involved in an opportunity where you can influence the future of the world by helping today's children develop their intellect, self-concept, and values. Imagine a program in which you can help people develop a lifelong zest for learning, love of reading, and the skills to be able to find the answers to their own questions. Adults working with children in infant/toddler programs have just that opportunity.

In order to help fulfill the promise of this opportunity this book will give ideas for sharing literature with the youngest of children and their parents.

How to use this book

Toddle On Over will first discuss the reasons for developing infant/toddler literature sharing programs. This introduction leads into a closer look at the stages of child development, then provides a suggested list of activities and books that are appealing at each level.

Effective techniques and successful samples of program formulas are offered to help you begin defining the program that will match your needs.

A collection of 53 thematic weekly programs that have been used successfully in our library follows this introductory material. Fingerplays and poems, patterns for story souvenirs and suggested story book titles are included in each. Planning thematic programs allows you to use creativity and imagination. The themes are mainly a tool to help tie things together. But, they also allow many opportunities for children to use speech, listening, and reading. The natural connections between these activities become more apparent to children when they are linked thematically. This approach also works well when a book is the starting place for ideas to go with it.

And finally, there are additional resources for special activities and professional development at the end of the book.

Infant/Toddler Time is a wonderful experience for child and parent. During Infant/Toddler Time, children learn to participate in games, fingerplays, rhymes, and songs, and learn how to sit and listen to good stories. It can be the first step towards a love of libraries, books, and reading that lasts a lifetime.

Acknowledgments

Thank you to the following contributors who supplied examples of exemplary infant/toddler program materials:

Judith Wilson
British Columbia Library Association
Young Adults and Children's Services
British Columbia, Canada

Cindy Christin, Children's Librarian
Bozeman Public Library
Bozeman, Montana

Betsy Diamant-Cohen, Librarian
Ruth Young Wing Feinstein Library
Israel Museum
Jerusalem, Israel

Elizabeth Draper, Youth Services
Euless Public Library, Euless, Texas

Lisa Falk, Children's Librarian
Los Angeles Public Library
Los Angeles, California

Susan Graf, Family Services Librarian
North Las Vegas Library District
North Las Vegas, Nevada
(Program developed at
Washoe County Library System
Reno, Nevada)

Helen Krejci, Children's Librarian
North Richland Hills Public Library
North Richland Hills, Texas

North Cleveland Library Consortium,
Northern Ohio Library Association, and
Northwest Library District Online,
Regional Library Systems, Ohio

Nan Nystrom-Hilk, Librarian
Rogers Library, Hennepin County Library
Rogers, Minnesota

Sigurd C. Rahmas
Story House Corporation
Charlottesville, NY

Kathleen Strauss
Emily Fowler Public Library
Denton Public Library System
Denton, Texas

Ellen G. Fader
Multnomah County Library
Portland, Oregon

Introduction to Infant/Toddler Programming

Why have programs for infants/toddlers?

An Infant/Toddler Time is a special time designed for children birth–35 months and their parents or caregivers that addresses the knowledge we now have about early learning. There are a few key statistics that can very quickly reveal the significance of programming for this age group. We now know, for example, that 50 percent of a person's intellectual capacity is developed before age four.[1] Additionally, children learn over 80 percent of the vocabulary that will serve them all of their lives by the time they are five.[2] It has also become apparent through recent research that learning occurs much earlier than was believed. From this type of evidence, more and more libraries are deciding to add programming to serve families during this critically important period in the language and intellectual development of children.

The list of key experiences below have been linked to the development of language and literacy.[3]

- having fun and early contact with language by listening to stories and rhyme, and seeing adults reading;
- talking about meaningful experiences;
- describing objects, events, letter names and sounds;
- writing and pre-writing, such as drawing, scribbling, and writing in conventional forms;
- dictating stories;
- reading in traditional and non-traditional ways ("reading" signs, logos, labels, and symbols, reading one's own writing, exploring picture books and reading-like play).

The natural fit with library storytimes is easy to see. And as you develop your Infant/Toddler Time, a list of benefits for children, families and the library grows and expands.

An infant/toddler time can do the following:

- Raise public awareness about the importance of the first three years of life.
- Educate parents and caregivers on ideas, quality literature, and techniques of interacting successfully with infant/toddlers.
- Entertain both children and parents/caregivers.
- Give a positive image to the library or group.
- Use the abundance material that is now published for this age group.
- Ready the children for regular storytime attendance when they reach the appropriate age.
- Promote family use of books, as well as family networking.
- Increase literature use by children, their parents, their grandparents in many cases, and their caregivers.
- Enrich the language experience of the children for better listening, vocabulary, thinking, and problem solving skills.
- Emphasize the institution's part, whether it is a library, preschool or other group, in the educational role of both parents and children.
- Provide the key experiences that lead to successful emergent literacy and language development.

Who are the toddlers? A developmental portrait

Infants and toddlers are active, into everything with a restless energy that amazes over and over again. *Do not* expect children of this age to sit quietly like older preschoolers. Be prepared for lots of noise and movement during sessions. It may at first feel like pandemonium working with this age—*but relax!* These children (and adults) are absorbing more than you think. What follows is a simple explanation of just what these children see, hear, and do. The charts on the next two pages show the development of infants and toddlers in one-year groupings for some easy comparisons.

Child Development Birth–4

Listening & Understanding	Communication	Motor & Movement	Literary Needs

Birth – One Year

Listening & Understanding	Communication	Motor & Movement	Literary Needs
Startles at loud noises. Listens to new sounds by stopping activity. Stops crying when spoken to and turns head to source of sound. Knows mother's voice. Responds to and plays with toys that make sound. Gurgles and coos	Has special, recognizable cries for hunger, pain, displeasure. Makes 30 seconds of eye contact when being spoken to. Responds to parent's voice when spoken to face-to-face. Makes cooing sounds. Laughs and smiles at a familiar person. Responds to an adult's tone rather than true meaning of words. Vocalizes to own image in mirror. May repeat one syllable over and over (ba-ba-ba). Imitates non-speech sounds such as smacking the lips. Begins to use gestures to communicate (bye-bye).	Lifts head when on parents shoulder or lying on stomach. Holds head erect with some bobbing when sitting. Clenches hand in fist. Rotates head. Plays with toy in one hand. Explores fingers and toys with mouth. Gives a first smile.	To develop awareness of communication. To hear language of any kind especially rhythmic rhymes, chants, and songs. To be stimulated to develop an interest in talking. To stimulate excitement about words. To touch, turn, chew on, and play with books.

One –Two Years

Listening & Understanding	Communication	Motor & Movement	Literary Needs
Understands and enjoys rhymes and songs. Recognizes own name. Responds to "no" when used emphatically by and adult. Recognizes the names of family members and a few familiar words. Understands simple directions such as "sit down." Recognizes names of more common objects and foods. Understands many more words that can say.	Imitates gestures such as "Patty Cake." Uses more gestures to communicate. Is developing a sense of humor and will laugh if a parent does. Vocalizes with music. Has use of exclamatory speech such as "uh-oh" or "ouch." Says first words ("mama," "dada," "bye") as related to a specific person or action. May use a word over and over. Uses "jargon talk."	Rolls over. Sits without support. Begins crawling. Begins to stand while pulling up and attempt to stand without help. Pushes, pulls, and bangs toys. Begins to walk sideways while holding furniture. Begins climbing. Scribbles with crayon or pencil. Crumples paper and opens packages.	To hear language of any kind, especially rhythmic, rhymes, chants, and songs. To participate in using repetitious books, point and name books, books that ask simple questions, books that have clear pictures of familiar objects, and books that have simple stories and predictable plots. To connect the tactile experience of an object with the name of the object.

Listening & Understanding	Communication	Motor & Movement	Literary Needs
Two –Three Years			
Enjoys having a familiar storybook read aloud.	Likes picture books, names pictures, and turns pages.	Climbs.	To hear language of any kind, especially rhythmic, rhymes, chants, and songs.
Can identify actions in pictures and remembers what comes next in familiar stories.	Protests by saying no.	Walks.	To participate in using repetitious books, point and name books, books that ask simple questions, books that have clear pictures of familiar objects, and books that have simple stories and predictable plots.
Vocabulary grows to over 300 words.	May make verbal requests ("More milk") and emphatic demands ("Tie my shoe.")	Runs.	
	Asks "why" frequently.	Takes lids off containers.	
Understands verbs and descriptive words.	Jargon speech drops away.	Dresses and undresses dolls.	
Understands and responds to simple questions.	Uses two word sentences.	Can jump and balance on one foot.	To respond to simple stories that can be dramatized, stories that feature families, important changes, and interesting characters.
Understands the quantity one.	Can imitate three word sentences.	Begins working simple puzzles.	
Understands "same" and can match like objects.	Uses pronouns and begins to use plurals.	Stacks small toys.	
		Kicks a ball and throws it overhand.	
		Likes to "help' with easy chores.	
Three–Four Years			
Understands who, what, where questions.	Uses past tense & overuses the -ed ending. ("It falled off.")	Climbs in and out of cars and chairs without assistance.	To hear language of any kind, especially rhythmic: rhymes, chants, & songs.
Understands more concepts, such as around, behind, in front of, and others.	Uses articles a and the correctly.	Rides a tricycle or bicycle with training wheels.	To participate in using repetitious books, point & name books, books that ask simple questions, books that have clear pictures of familiar objects, and books that have stories with predictable plots.
Understands the names of familiar places. (Grandma's house, outside, the store)	Will make a choice when asked a question. ("Do you like pink or blue?")	Can walk on tiptoe.	
	Speaks in sentences of three or more words.	Can string beads.	
Understands & responds to the concept of taking turns.		Can copy a circle on paper.	
Knows name, sex, and age.	Vocabulary may be close to 1000 words.	Holds and uses a pencil with good control	To respond to simple stories that can be dramatized, stories that feature families, important changes, and interesting characters.
Listens and can be reasoned with verbally.	Tells about recent experiences.		
Understands more descriptive words.	Plays with words and says funny things on purpose.		To retell stories and to use characters from books in dramatic play.
	Tries to control situations by using words. ("I don't want to!")		

Reading Development

Narrowing our view now to the reading behaviors children exhibit at different age levels will be a helpful tool in choosing and using age-appropriate materials. The lists below are divided into three age ranges. Each suggests picture book titles that are appropriate for the age group. Following the list of titles are some of the book behaviors you can expect to see. And finally, under the heading "Do this" are suggestions for motions, activities and props that will work well with each age. Some of these are further divided into subgroupings within the age range.

Suggested Books: Age 0–12 Months

Anholt, Catherine. *Here Come the Babies.* Candlewick, 1993.

Greenfield, Monica. *The Baby.* HarperCollins, 1994.

Henderson, Kathy. *Bumpity Bump.* Candlewick, 1994.

Hoban, Tana. *Black On White.* Greenwillow, 1993.

Kemp, Moria. *Round and Round the Garden.* Lodestar, 1992.

Leslie, Amanda. *Play, Kitten, Play.* Candlewick, 1993.

McDonnel, Flora. *I Love Animals.* Candlewick, 1994.

Omerod, Jan. *To Baby With Love.* Lothrop, 1994.

Paterson, Bettina. *My First Animals.* Crowell, 1990.

Book behaviors for:
Handles books. Crumbles, tears, and chews books. Ignores print, but stares at pictures.

Do this:
Give children board, cloth, and plastic books to experience.

Interact with child through lullabies, facial expressions, songs, and touching.

Practice grasping, pulling, kicking, and other movement through action rhymes and fingerplays.

Point and name objects in books and life.

Bring real objects for sharing.

Repeat favorite songs and stories.

Encourage verbal participation.

Suggested Books: Age 12–24 Months

Alborough, Jez. *Where's My Teddy?* Candlewick, 1992.

Brown, Laurene. *Toddler Time.* Joy Street, 1990.

Goennel, Heidi. *My Dog.* Orchard, 1989.

Hoban, Tana. *Look Up, Look Down.* Orchard, 1989.

Isadora, Rachel. *I See.* Greenwillow, 1991.

Tafuri, Nancy. *Have You Seen My Duckling?* Greenwillow, 1994.

Wells, Rosemary. *Shy Charles.* Dial, 1988.

Ziefert, Harriet. *Baby Ben Gets Dressed.* Random House, 1985.

Book behaviors for: 12–15 Months
Turns pages of book in random order.

Verbalizes while pointing to pictures.

Points to pictures of known objects when objects are named.

Pats pictures of favorite things.

Identifies round things, such as a ball, circle, the letter "O."

Do this:
Pass items for sharing among the group.

Introduce concepts, such as colors, letters, and numbers.

Use flannelboard and chalkboard tell and draw stories.

Things You Will Want to Do Often

- Whisper, coo, and talk to the very young child.
- Sing a variety of songs.
- Name items aloud.
- Recite fingerplays.
- Tape record child's voice and play back.
- Let the child explore your mouth with his or her hands as you talk.
- Have writing and drawing materials available.
- Provide musical instruments or toys that make noise.

- Talk expressively.
- Describe activities as you do them.
- Read aloud enthusiastically.
- Let child talk on a real or play telephone.
- Have one-on-one conversations with children.
- Provide an environment that has an abundance of reading materials available.
- Listen to recordings of good books.

Book behaviors for: 15–18 months

Places picture in line of vision.

Asks for pictures of objects to be named.

Tells a "story" in reference to pictures on a page.

Answers questions about familiar stories that have been read aloud repeatedly.

Shows concern for the condition of books.

Guesses at the outcome of new stories.

Do this:

Use longer stories and activities.

Introduce the element of surprise.

Allow for questions and verbalizations.

Book behaviors for: 18–24 Months

Has a favorite book.

Pretends to read.

Turns pages from right to left.

Asks for stories to be read.

Remains attentive as stories are read.

Remembers names of characters in stories.

Do this:

Tell oral stories with simple story lines using familiar object props.

Include a show and tell time in program.

Allow children to choose favorite books to be included in programs.

Suggested Books: Age 24–36 Months

Bornstein, Ruth. *Little Gorilla.* Seabury, 1976.

Bunting, Eve. *Flower Garden.* Harcourt Brace Jovanovich, 1994.

Dodds, Ann Dayle. *Wheel Away.* Harper & Row, 1989.

Galdone, Paul. *The Gingerbread Boy.* Seabury, 1975.

Goode, Diane. *Where's Our Mama?* Dutton, 1991.

McMillan, Bruce. *Play Day.* Henry Holt, 1991.

Wood, Audrey. *The Napping House.* Harcourt Brace Jovanovich, 1984.

Book behaviors for: 24–30 Months

Knows the front, back, top and bottom of a book.

Enjoys looking through picture books.

Likes hearing and repeating rhymes and songs.

Talks to book characters.

Completes oral sentences when a word is left out.

Repeats sentences verbatim.

Reacts emotionally to stories.

Asks for books on particular subjects to be read (dinosaurs, horses, etc.).

Notices capital letters when they are in a contrasting color.

Do this:

Use books with fun, colorful, or unusual lettering.

Encourage group interaction.

Give assignments to parent and child for next program time.

Allow children to choose theme for future programs.

Book behaviors for: 30–36 Months

Remains attentive when a story is read even if no pictures are present.

Can choose pictures that are the same.

Can relate activities in the order which they occurred.

Can name some of the letters in own name.

Asks to see pictures when listening to a story.

Do this:

Include marching activities in program.

Include dance activities in program.

Include guessing or matching books in program.

Books should have:

1. Familiar content Present themes that are part of the child's world, such as everyday activities or building a sense of trust.

2. Large, colorful or well defined, uncluttered illustrations.

3. Simple and linear plots and few characters: Not all books for the infant/toddler are stories, but when the book does have a discernable plot, it should be straightforward and avoid tangents. *Rosie's Walk* by Pat Hutchins (Macmillan, 1971) is an excellent example of a good, clear plot. The story should also come to a swift resolution and end on a positive note.

4. Repetitive words or actions, cumulation, or participation features.

5. Elements that can lead to other creative activities such as fingerplays, songs, or creative dramatics.

6. Manipulative features such as flaps, tabs, etc. These work extremely well with this age. This type of book has built in child participation that help keep their attention.

Notes

1. Dorothy Butler, *Babies Need Books*, Athenaeum, 1980, p.1.

2. Judy Nichols, *Storytimes for Two Year Olds*, ALA, 1987.

3. Betsy Evans, "Extensions," September, 1996, p. 1&4.

Developmentally Appropriate Practice

Developmentally appropriate practice (DAP) is described by the National Association for the Education of Young Children and he Association for Childhood Education International as applying what we know about how young children develop to the activities, language and practices that we do with them. The knowledge about child development comes from accumulated data and facts that many experts have compiled from directly observing, testing and working with children. DAP is not a curriculum, but it is an approach to interacting with children in a way that considers their physical, emotional, social, and cognitive growth. But DAP does not use the opinions that experts write about exclusively. Rather, it combines the observations of the adult who is working with a group of kids about such things as culture, community expectations, family circumstances, and individual preferences. While DAP is age appropriate practice, the adult leader adds the element of individually appropriate practice. This is actually a pretty straightforward, common sense idea—find out as much as you can about the age group and the individuals in that group and plan accordingly.

For further reading on Developmentally Appropriate Practice

Bredenkamp, Sue. (editor) *Developmentally Appropriate Practice in Early Childhood Programs Serving Children From Birth Through Age 8.* National Association for the Education of Young Children, 1987.

Elkind, D. "Developmentally Appropriate Practice: Philosophical and Practical Implications." *Phi Delta Kappan*, October, 1989, 113-117.

Gestwicki, Carol. *Developmentally Appropriate Practice: Curriculum and Development in Early Education.* Delamr Publishers, 1995.

Kostelnik, M.J. "Recognizing the Essentials of Developmentally Appropriate Practice." *Child Care Information Exchange*, March, 1993, 73-77.

Strickland, Dorothy and L.M. Morrow. (editors) *Emerging Literacy: Young Children Learn to Read and Write.* International Reading Association, 1989.

Young, Kathryn T. *Staring Points: Meeting the Needs of Our Youngest Children.* Carnegie Corporation, 1994.

Creating Your Infant/Toddler Program

Before You Begin Your Program

Visit another program

Find someone in a nearby community who already has experience with this age group and arrange to go observe them in action! This will show you that the program can work, as well as how it can be done.

Assess yourself

The following is a list to use in assessing yourself if you will be the leader of an Infant/Toddler Literature Program.

⚫ Prepare the rest of your staff

An infant/toddler program is not a quiet event! Make sure the rest of the staff of your organization is aware and prepared for the active and noisy group. This is especially important if you will be holding the program in an open area of your building.

⚫ Schedule an appropriate time

Because of the sleeping and eating schedules of infant/toddlers, perhaps the best time to hold a program is mid-morning. An early evening or Saturday program would also include those adults who have other employment.

⚫ Do careful planning

Infant/toddler sessions must be carefully planned to be successful. Plan a variety of activities, especially those with movement, music, and participation. Activities and stories must go quickly, include lots of movement, sound and concrete items to keep the children's attention. Use stories and other activities that are familiar to you. If possible, run through each element of the program using a stopwatch. This will ensure that you plan enough activities to fill the desired time frame.

⚫ Choose a good setting

Plan to hold your infant/toddler sessions in an area with a minimum of distractions. The most important things to remember are the setting must:

- Be kid friendly and baby safe. Cover all outlets and sharp table corners. Discard all objects smaller than 1⅜" in diameter.
- Have display tables. Feature board books; point-and-name books; manipulative books; touch and feel books; nursery rhymes; songs; Mother Goose books; picture books; fingerplay, hand game or movement books; and parenting books.
- Be at baby eye level. It is best to have the adults sit on the floor with the child, while the presenter is on a low chair or stage.
- Provide stroller space
- Provide a baby changing table close and accessible to both the father and mother.
- Provide bright colors and attention-getting objects in your sharing area. Play music while children and adults enter to create a welcoming, sound rich environment.

⚫ Have a buddy

If it is possible to have an assistant or co-leader for your infant/toddler program, do so! Having someone with you will allow freedom during the program, because whoever is not presenting will be able to assist attendees, make out nametags for late-comers, help capture escaping babies, etc. If you can find a professional or volunteer who has a special talent such as playing an instrument, this will also add to the variety of the program.

⚫ Set guidelines

A strict set of rules is not necessary when both child and adult are present. A set of general guidelines will also allow you the flexibility needed to deal with this age group.

⚫ Ask for participation of adults

Encourage the participation of adults by telling them

to interact with the child. Giving them copies of fingerplays or songs to take home will encourage them to repeat the activities at home. Tell the adults who come to prepare the infant/toddler by talking to them directly about what will and did happen in the program.

↝ Have registration

The programs suggested here can be used effectively for groups of adults and infant/toddlers up to about 40 people. The ideal size is about 20. (Ten adults and ten children.) Because of the size limitation, it might be a good idea to preregister children for the program. This will also ensure that the program will be well attended. If you have a list of kids, their adults and phone numbers, you can also call and remind them they are registered to attend and tell them about upcoming events. Registration also allows you to talk with the adults who will be attending and inform them of their role in your program.

↝ Make nametags

Some who work with infant/toddler programs like to have nametags. Addressing children by their name helps capture their attention. Nametags also add a personal note as you learn the names of both parent and child. A drawback is that most nametags on children end up on the floor or in the child's mouth. Try giving the adult a nametag with both parent and child's name on it, or sticking an adhesive nametag to the child's back.

↝ Look for support groups

Infant/toddler programs often have a great deal of community support and appreciation. The program leader will get to know the adults and children who attend personally. When people become involved personally, it is much easier to get them to support a program with votes or money.

↝ Have flexibility and variety

Infant/toddlers do not always respond to books and activities in the way we would like. Since these children tend to be egocentric, they do not remember rules and will interrupt. Be prepared for the inevitable interruptions. Plan for and allow wandering. Be prepared to stop the story and sing a song if the group is very restless. Modify your activities based on the audience mood. Having a program with lots of variety will help hold the young child's attention. Use a new song, a puppet, or a musical instrument. Invite a special guest or animal guest. Add a coloring sheet or game. The possibilities are endless!

↝ Make activity sheets

The 53 themed programs have been created so they can be used as activity sheets. Use them as:

1. Cheat sheet to guide you through the program.
2. An outline to promote audience participation
3. A learning tool for parent or caregiver

↝ Think About Group Experiences

A successful group literature experience would have the following qualities:

Children are active and participate in speech and/or motor involvement.

The leader is enthusiastic and this is communicated to the participants through facial expressions and manner.

Surefire Attention Getters for Starting Your Program

These activities get the group focused, settle them for the first story, encourage participation, and set the mood. Some good attention getters are:

A Bell
Softly ring a bell or jingle your keys as a signal that the program is beginning.

A Puppet Host
Bring your small, gentle-looking puppet out of a special box or basket (where it has been "sleeping")

Fingerplays or Action Rhymes:
These attention getters provide a transition between stories. They can be repeated as often as needed. Fingerplays and action rhymes also help expel toddler energy before a story.

The leader is prepared and has all the materials needed at her fingertips.

The leader and group are accepting of children's feelings and participation.

The activities are developmentally appropriate to the particular group.

The leader provides clear and purposeful clarification of new concepts.

Some of the activities included are previously learned and familiar material.

The atmosphere is relaxed and does not pressure or threaten children.

For further information on assessing your program see "How Good is Your Infant Program?" by Alice Honig and Ronald Lally. *Child Care Quarterly* 4(3): 137-39.)

Opening Story Sessions

The opening and closing activities are important one. You want to catch you audience's attention with the opening fingerplay or rhyme, let them know it is time to settle down to listen, and provide a familiar and friendly beginning for the action to follow. Some good openers are:

Opening Action Rhymes:

Wiggles Out

I wiggle my fingers,
I wiggle my toes,
I wiggle my shoulders,
I wiggle my nose.
Now no more wiggles
Are left in me
And I will be
As still as can be.
(*do actions as described*)

Wiggles, II

A wiggle, wiggle here,
A wiggle, wiggle there.
Wiggle your hands,
Up in the air.
Wiggle your shoulders,
Wiggle your hips,
Wiggle your knees,
and move your lips.
Wiggle, wiggle wiggle,
And wiggle and bend.
Wiggle, wiggle, wiggle,
And this is the end!

Two Little Hands

Two little hands go clap, clap, clap.
Two little feet go tap, tap, tap.
Two little fists go thump, thump, thump.
Two little legs go jump, jump, jump.
One little body turns around,
And everyone sits quietly down.
(*do actions as described*)

Here is My Book

Here is my book,
I open it wide
To see the pictures
That are inside.

Closing the Sessions

When it is time to go, you want to send everyone off with a warm and friendly ending:

Closing poem: *We've Listened*

We've listened to stories
And sat with our friends,
But now we are finished
And it is *THE END*.

And for those times when things get too noisy:

Action rhyme to quiet the group: Tiny Mouse

There is such a tiny mouse,
  living quietly in my house.
Out at night he starts to creep,
  when everyone is fast asleep.
But always by the light of day,
  the mouse quietly, quietly creeps away.

Other Elements to Add to Storytime

Puppets

Puppets allow toddlers to get close to the group leader through the puppet. Puppets also help with leaving—kids hug it goodbye, look forward to seeing puppet next time.

Music

Toddlers love to sing. Songs and music help when the group is restless-a song will draw their attention in. Music also develops listening and auditory skills, and sets the tone for an enjoyable session

Visual props and flannelboard stories

Props provide a concrete story experience. Flannel stories add visual variety.

Story souvenirs

Story souvenirs are tangible items that children take from the infant/toddler session to help them remember what the stories, fingerplays, songs and activities were about. These items are not crafts for the children to do, but are made ahead of time.

Big books

Many of the books listed in the bibliographies are available in big book format. Big books are especially useful if you have large groups, or simply want the bigger pictures to help hold the children's attention.

Pop-up and movable books: My Big Secret

Of all the items that I have used in working with infants and toddlers, pop-up and movable books have been by far the most effective and fun. The caregivers and the parents *love* to watch you lift the flaps—over and over! The pop-up pictures bring squeals of delight from adults and children alike. Many of the books in the bibliography are lift-the-flap, toy, or movable books. The annotations indicate which books have these features.

Infant/Toddler Program Formulas
Programs That Work

Programs for adults who live or work with children who are age birth to three years are being done with significant frequency. A variety of formats are being done with success. These are intended as participatory teaching experiences for both adult and child. At these programs, leaders introduce adults and children to a wide variety of language experiences, most commonly using picture books, flannelboard stories, fingerplays, action rhymes, movement, music, educational play, puppets and media. Because of what we know about children, we know that infant/toddler programs require careful planning. We know the books chosen must be short with simple plots and large colorful or clear pictures. We know a variety of activities will help keep the child's attention, as long as they are short, sometimes physical, and familiar.

Organize your infant/toddler materials in any of the following "kid-tested" formulas, which are being used by program leaders across the United States.

Here is some advice from practicing librarians:

"I did let the lapsit kids get down and explore—our room is as childproof as we can make it. We sit in a circle, with me slightly above the others (so they can see). I sit on a kick stool. Between each brief title, we do a fingerplay or song, the same three or four each time bearing in mind that toddlers love repetition. I use a little rubber hand puppet tyrannosaurus as a mascot to break the ice. He is very shy and would cower on my neck as I told about his shyness. I asked the children if they would like to pet him. After giving all the children an opportunity to pet him, I would ask him if he were ready to listen. He would nod "yes" and I would put him in my pocket and begin. I brought him back out to say goodbye." —Mary H. Atlanta Fulton Public Library

"We love doing Mother Goose laptimes. We have a fairly structured program for about 15-20 minutes, then we always have a few manipulatives for the babies to play with at the end. We have nerf balls, tennis balls, beach balls, long tubes or boxes for crawling through, formula cans and clothespins (kids love the sound the clothespins make when dropped in the cans). Sometimes we have huge sheets of paper and chunky crayons, puppets, or ziplock bags with jello to squish." — Cathy W., Columbus Metropolitan Library

Formula 1
Infant/Toddler Time,
Hurst Public Library, Hurst, TX
Approximately 30 minutes. Programs held weekly.

Welcome: Puppet host comes out and introduces theme.

Action rhyme: *Wiggles Out* (see p. 15 for rhyme)

Action rhyme: *Grandma's Glasses*
(stand and sit at the end)
Here are grandma's glasses,
(make small glasses with hands)
Here is grandma's hat.
(make small hat with hands)
This is the way she folds her hands, (fold hands)
And puts them in her lap.
Here are grandpa's glasses, *(make large glasses)*
Here is grandpa's hat.
(make large hat)
This is the way he folds his arms, (fold arms)
And sits like that. (sit)

Opening poem: *Here Is My Book*

Here is my book, I open it wide
To see the pictures that are inside.
(hold hands together as if holding closed book, then open hands as if opening book)

Story 1: Book

Fingerplay

Story 2: Flannel or prop story

Song

Story 3: Book

Puppet host passes out souvenirs and greets each child.

Story 4: Book (if time permits)

Tell them about next weeks theme or stories.

Closing poem: *We've Listened to Stories* (see p. 15)
Puppet host says goodbye and gives hugs at door.

Formula 2
Book Babies,
Marshall Public Library, Pocatello, ID
Approximately 30 minutes. Programs held monthly.

Five to ten minutes: A basket of board books are set out in the middle of the floor in the program area. Children are allowed to freely "interact" with the books.

Twenty minutes: A guest speaker addresses topics of concern to adults living or working with young children. Topics include CPR, Age Appropriate Toys, Positive parenting, etc.

Formula 3
Mother Goose Laptime,
Columbus Metropolitan Main Library,
Columbus, OH
Approximately 20 minutes. Programs held monthly.

Fifteen minutes: Various rhymes, songs, fingerplays, and Mother Goose rhymes.

Five minutes: Sharing of one to two board books.

Closing song: "Baby Hop" from *Diaper Gym Cassette*, Kimbo Educational.

Formula 4
First Friends,
Monroe Public Library, Monroe, IN
Approximately 30 minutes. Programs held weekly.

This formula is held in a "mini-center" in the library that is filled with age-appropriate board books,
books, music and fingerplay cassettes. The center is reserved for the infant/toddlers and their adults for sessions of self-directed, one-on-one interaction.

Formula 5
First Friends,
Monroe Public Library, Monroe, IN
Approximately 30 minutes. Programs held weekly.

Song

Story 1: Book

Four action rhymes or fingerplays

Story 2: Cloth book

Story 3: Book

Repeat four rhymes

Song

Ten minutes: Creative activity or personal interaction with music cassettes and recorders.

Formula 6
Warren Memorial Library,
Warren, ME
Approximately 30 minutes. Programs held weekly at under two daycare sites.

Opening song

Passive rhyme

Book 1

Active rhyme

Active song

Passive rhyme

Book 2

Closing song

Formula 7
Finger Fun Babies,
Portland Public Library, Portland, ME
Approximately 20 minutes. Programs held weekly.

Mother Goose rhyme

Mother Goose rhyme

Fingerplay

Song with actions

Fingerplay

Song with actions

Parent socialize

Baby book buckets

Formula 8
Mother Goose on the Loose,
Betsy Diamant-Cohen, Israel Museum
Approximately 30 minutes. Programs held weekly.

Warm up: 10 minutes

Mother Goose rhymes (3): One with a flannel board and one with a book or song.

Movement: Five minutes

Action songs

Participation rhymes

Closing song

Formula 9
Babies and Books,
Nan Nystrom-Hilk,
Rogers Library, Rogers, MN
Programs held weekly.

Puppet greeting

Basket of board books for exploration

Picture books, songs, rhymes, videos

Formula 10
Books and Babies,
Bozeman Public Library, Bozeman, MT
Programs held twice weekly.

Opening songs

Chants, rhymes, lap games & movement: 15 minutes

Closing song: "Twinkle, Twinkle Little Star"

Infant/toddler play: 30 minutes

Baskets of infant/toddler toys are distributed. Children play for under the supervision of their adult. Parents network, and the group leader models play activities.

TODDLER Acronym

I developed this acronym to help you to remember the developmental state of children 18–36 months old and the implications for practice with them.

Talkative A toddler will talk and talk and talk—all through toddler storytime if you let him. Toddlers will listen to stories for a short while, play pretend games, and recount their day in detail.
   What to do: Verbal interactive time should be allowed before, during and after toddler storytimes.

On their own way Toddlers are interested in the here and now. They cannot comprehend the moral of stories about death or illness, and can't do many arts and craft projects.
   What to do: Use books with familiar stories, repeating rhymes and words, flannel boards and fingerplays.

Dependent and independent Sometimes very bold and independent, other times, hiding behind mom.
   What to do: Make sure a parent, relative, or caregiver remains with each child.

Different Toddlers have a wide range of developmental interests and abilities—much wider than the chronological age range of the group would suggest.
   What to do: Be prepared! Allow for children who exhibit unusual interests or abilities.

Loving Toddlers have an increased awareness of their own feelings. These feelings are exhibited most positively in pride of creation, expression of feelings in symbolic play (hugs), and empathetic concern for others.
   What to do: Have a host puppet that is huggable. Be warmly responsive to toddlers needs & have patience.

Everywhere *Toddlers are so active!* They have just become mobile, and want to get at all objects everywhere.
   What to do: Plan a variety of activities, including songs, fingerplays, action rhymes, story interactions, participations, etc. Hold toddler storytimes in an area where there are a minimum of distractions.

Responsive Toddlers learn through engagement. Touching, tasting, feeling, observing, and hearing.
   What to do: Provide participation activities. Use manipulates, masks, stuffed objects. Pass them around.

Selfish Toddlers are egocentric. They frequently want their own way, do not share, interrupt during stories.
   What to do: Be sure to have enough of whatever activity you are going to do (art supplies, props, etc.) for each child. Use redirecting, ignoring, and incorporating.

Announcements and Handouts

There are many ways you can support your program with announcements and handouts. The samples here suggest some of the most important ways to communicate with parents and caregivers.

Announcing your program and attracting your audience is the first order of business.

The Bozeman Public Library
and
Prevent Child Abuse, Inc.

present

"The Busy Parent's
Guide
to Toddlers"

A Six-Week Workshop Based on the Bestselling Book
"How to Talk So Kids Will Listen and
Listen So Kids Will Talk"
by Adele Faber and Elaine Mazlish

Plea...

BABIES
&
BOOKS!

MOTHER GOOSE TIME
For Pre-Walkers
Fridays, Oct. 4, 11, 18, 25

TODDLER TALES
For Walkers to Age 36 Months
Fridays, Nov. 1, 8, 15, 22

SPACE LIMITED!
Contact Lisa Falk,
Children's Librarian, to register!

Westchester Branch Library
8946 Sepulveda Eastway
310-645-6082

The Ruth Youth Wing
The Israel Museum, Jerusalem

Are you home in the morning with your children, looking for something fun to do?

Come join us at:

Mother Goose
n the Loose

...ery rhyme program
s 1–5 with
...iamant-Cohen

fee: 10 shekels
call: 6708952 for further information

at the Grete Fraenkel-Meydam Reading Room,
of the Ruth Youth Wing Feinstein Library,

Flyers used with permission from the Bozeman Public Library, Bozeman, Montana; Westchester Branch Library, Los Angeles, California; and the Ruth Young Wing Feinstein Library, Jerusalem, Israel.

FAMILY LITERACY:

THE A B Cs OF THE PARENT'S ROLE IN READING

FAMILY SERVICES
NORTH LAS VEGAS LIBRARY DISTRICT
2300 CIVIC CENTER DRIVE
NORTH LAS VEGAS, NEVADA
633 1070

UNPR[...]
You [...]
chil[...]
the [...]
Be [...]

VALU[...]
Bec[...]
sho[...]
and [...]
see [...]
rea[...]
the [...]
be [...]

WRITI[...]
Wri[...]
Wri[...]
mar[...]
avail[...]
wan[...]
exp[...]
jour[...]
for [...]

X TRA[...] EXPERIENCES
Your role in early reading requires you to devote extra attention to your children's needs and help with their first encounters with print. You can obtain help from books such as <u>The Read Aloud Handbook</u> (Trelease, 1982) and <u>A Parent's Guide to Children's Reading</u> (Larrick, 1982).

YOUR LITERATE HOME
Create a nurturing and literate environment for your young child to learn and grow in. The experiences in your home can make a difference in your child's reading development.

ZOO TRIPS
Zoo trips, museums, amusement parks, and community parks are places that you can visit with your child. Visits to these special places engage your child in new experiences to learn from and talk about. These experiences can be extended by using children's literature before and after the visits.

The Family Literacy brochure is an example of an information handout. Simple and helpful suggestions for parents on supporting their child's learning and coping with parenting stresses are two popular topics that can really make a difference for families. Used with permission of the North Las Vegas District Library.

This parent's page below is an example of a take-home sheet. A nice reminder of the program that allows parents to reinforce the fingerplays and activities learned during the Infant/Toddler Program. Used with permission of the Euless Public Library, Euless, Texas.

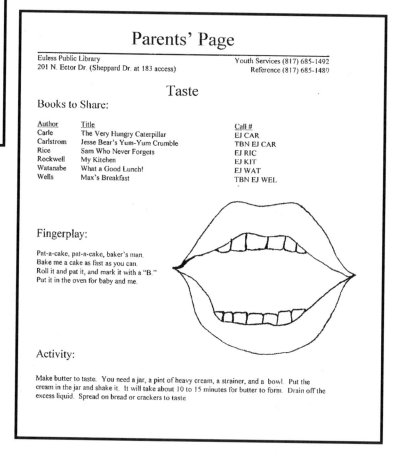

Parents' Page

Euless Public Library
201 N. Ector Dr. (Sheppard Dr. at 183 access)

Youth Services (817) 685-1492
Reference (817) 685-1489

Taste

Books to Share:

Author	Title	Call #
Carle	The Very Hungry Caterpillar	EJ CAR
Carlstrom	Jesse Bear's Yum-Yum Crumble	TBN EJ CAR
Rice	Sam Who Never Forgets	EJ RIC
Rockwell	My Kitchen	EJ KIT
Watanabe	What a Good Lunch!	EJ WAT
Wells	Max's Breakfast	TBN EJ WEL

Fingerplay:

Pat-a-cake, pat-a-cake, baker's man.
Bake me a cake as fast as you can.
Roll it and pat it, and mark it with a "B."
Put it in the oven for baby and me.

Activity:

Make butter to taste. You need a jar, a pint of heavy cream, a strainer, and a bowl. Put the cream in the jar and shake it. It will take about 10 to 15 minutes for butter to form. Drain off the excess liquid. Spread on bread or crackers to taste.

53 Themed Programs

The programs on pp. 21–88 were designed to be used with formula 1 (p. 16), but could easily be adapted for some of the other formulas described in this chapter. The book suggestions for each activity are age appropriate and theme related, but usually you will need only three to four books per session (fewer if the children are younger than 18 months). To make selection of books easier, those titles best-suited for infants are indicated with an (I) following the annotation. You may also refer back to formula 1 for a suggested order and length for your program. With this information you can begin building your library's wonderfully successful Infant/Toddler Program.

All About Me

Carlson, Nancy. *I Like Me!* Puffin, 1993. Louanne Pig extolls the virtues of being best friends with herself.

Cauley, Lorinda. *Clap Your Hands.* Putnam, 1992. Rhyming text instructs the listener to perform playful actions with human and animal characters pictured.

Greenfield, Eloise. *Big Friend, Little Friend.* Writers and Readers, 1991. Sensitive illustrations and simple text celebrate the riches of friendship in an African American family.

Holzenthaler, Jean. *My Hands Can.* Dutton, 1978. This book describes the simple activities that hands can do.

Martin, Bill. *Here Are My Hands.* Lothrop, 1987. Children see a variety of colored animals in this repetitive text.

Melmed, Laura. *I Love You As Much...* Lothrop, 1993. A variety of mothers, animal and human, let their children know how much they love them.

Priddy, Roger. *Baby's Book of the Body.* Dorling Kindersley, 1993. A photographic introduction to the body for very young children.

I Have a Nose

On my face, I have a nose,
(touch nose)
And way down here, I have ten toes.
(touch toes)
I have two eyes that I can blink,
(point to eyes)
I have a head to help me think.
(point to head)
I have a chin and very near,
(point to chin)
I have two ears so I can hear.
(point to ears)
Here are my arms to hold up high,
(raise arms over head)
And here is my hand to wave goodbye.
(wave)
[Fingerplay]

My Friend Has a Face

(To the tune of "Old MacDonald.")

My friend _____ has a face,
(substitute child's name)
E-I-E-I-O.
And on her face she has a nose,
E-I-E-I-O.
With a sniff, sniff here,
And a sniff, sniff there,
Here a sniff, there a sniff,
Everywhere a sniff, sniff
My friend _____ has a face,
E-I-E-I-O!

Repeat with two eyes (blink) and mouth (smile).
[Song]

My Fingers

My fingers can stand up straight and tall.
(hold fingers tall)
My fingers can bend and be very small.
(bend fingers)
My fingers can clasp my hands in a ball
(make one fist and clasp with other hand)
My fingers can jump, my fingers can fall.
[Fingerplay]

☺ **Story Souvenir:** <u>All About Me Book</u>

Enlarge and photocopy the cover for booklet. Add baby's name in the blank. Make additional pages for handprint, footprint and age. Staple down the side.

All About Me

_____

♡

Animal Sounds

Boynton, Sandra. *But Not the Hippopotamus.* Little Simon, 1992. A group of common animals have fun together—but not the hippopotamus!

Dodds, Dayle Ann. *Do Bunnies Talk?* Harper Collins, 1992. This book introduces a variety of human and animal sounds that bunnies do not make.

Fleming, Denise. *Barnyard Banter.* Holt, 1994. All of the barnyard animals are where they should be, each making their own distinctive sound except for the goose.

Hudson, Cheryl. *Animal Sounds for Baby.* Scholastic Inc., 1996. Appealing African American babies listen to animal sounds through rhymed text.

Kuskin, Karla. *Roar and More.* Harper & Row, 1990. Rhymed text presents the behavior and noises of various zoo animals.

Martin, Bill. *Polar Bear, Polar Bear, What Do You Hear?* Henry Holt, 1983. Children hear a variety of noisy animal sounds at the zoo. *Note: Make animal masks when sharing this story.*

Most, Bernard. *The Cow That Went OINK!* Harcourt Brace Jovanovich, 1990. A cow that oinks and a pig that moos are ridiculed by the other barnyard animals until they teach one another something.

Polushkin, Maria. *Who Said Meow?* Bradbury, 1978. A cute puppy tries to find the source of a new sound he hears.

Who's That

Growl, growl,
Thud, thud, *(slap floor)*
Roar, roar,
Who's that knocking on the door?
Pound, pound, *(hit floor)*
Stamp, stamp,
Scratch, scratch, *(make scratching motion)*
Who's that wiggling at the latch?
Can a pig be at my door? *(oink)*
No, pigs don't roar!
Can a cow be wiggling my latch? *(moo)*
No, cows can't scratch.
Roar, roar,
Scratch, scratch,
Growl, growl,
It's not an owl, *(hoot)*
I know who it can be,
A friendly lion is visiting me! *(point to self)*
[Action Rhyme]

Pretend

I'm a cat—hear me meow,
I'm an alligator—hear me roar.
I'm a duck—hear me quack,
As I'm running out the door.
(hold up three, two, and one finger)
[Fingerplay]

Animal Sound Game

Obtain a pre-recorded tape of animal sounds, or make a tape of yourself imitating the animal sounds. Play the tape for your group and have fun guessing the animal.

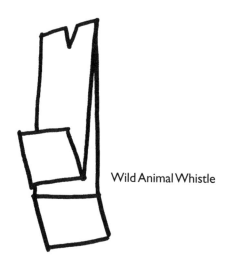

Wild Animal Whistle

☼ **Story Souvenir:** Wild Animal Whistle
Materials: Very thin paper, scissors
Cut long strips of thin paper in any width and length. Fold the strip in half and make a crease. Fold one end of the strip up and crease. Fold the other end down and crease. Snip out a small notch in the center of the middle fold. Hold the wild animal whistle loosely between two fingers. Close the folded ends. Put the paper against your lips and blow hard.

Babies

(I) Indicates books for infants.

Anholt, Catherine. *Here Come the Babies.* Candlewick, 1993. Rhymed text tells about the behavior of babies as seen through the eyes of older siblings. (I)

Ellwand, David. *The Big Book of Beautiful Babies.* Dutton, 1995. Black and white photographs with simple rhymed text show beautiful babies. (I)

Kingman, Lee. *Catch the Baby.* Viking, 1990. A rambunctious toddler is on the run exploring things in this rhyming tale.

Omerod, Jan. *To Baby With Love.* Lothrop, 1994. An illustrated collection of rhymes for babies featuring "Turtle" and "What Are We to Do?" (I)

Paxton, Tom. *Where's the Baby?* Morrow, 1993. After looking all over the house for the baby, the reader finds her in a very safe place.

Pearson, Susan. *When Baby Went to Bed.* Viking Kestrel, 1987. One by one, ten animals climb into a baby's crib at bedtime. *Note: Collect stuffed animals or puppets and a blanket to act out this book.* (I)

Reasoner, Charles. *Who's My Baby?* Dorling Kindersley, 1997. A big board book packed with recognizable photographs of animals and animal babies. (I)

Schwartz, Amy. *A Teeny Tiny Baby.* Orchard, 1994. A very small baby describes his favorite activities.

Stein, Holly Ann. *Oh, Baby!* Walker, 1993. Text and color photographs describe what babies do. (I)

Wilds, Kazumi. *Hajime in the North Woods.* Little Brown, 1994. Baby Hajime spends a wonderful night with the animals in the woods, but returns home to his parents in the morning.

Baby Grows
(Point to body parts as indicated.)

Five little fingers on this hand,
Five little fingers on that.
A dear little nose,
A mouth like a rose,
Two little cheeks so fat.
Two eyes, two ears,
And ten little toes.
We'll watch the baby every day
To see how fast he grows!
[Action Rhyme]

Five Little Babies
Use the pattern for the I Love My Baby bookmark to create a flannel board. Trace the baby five times on Pellon (interfacing) and color with colored pencils. Cut them out and you have a flannel board.

One little baby rocking in a tree *(rock arms)*
Two little babies splashing in the sea
(pretend to swim)
Three little babies crawling on the floor,
(pretend to crawl)
Four little babies banging on the door
("knock" on pretend door)
Five little babies playing hide and seek
(peek through fingers)
Keep your eyes closed until I say *PEEK!*
(take hands away)
[Action Rhyme]

Music: "Rock-a-Bye Baby" from *Wee Sing Nursery Rhymes and Lullabies* by Pam Beall. Price Stern Sloan, 1985.

☼ **Story Souvenir:** I Love My Baby bookmark Photocopy and enlarge the pattern onto stiff white paper and cut to 3½" x 6". Color the heart red on each bookmark.

Bathtime

Allen, Pamela. *Mr. Archimedes Bath.* HarperCollins, 1993. Mr. Archimede cannot figure out who is spilling water from his bathtub.

Kundra, C.I. *To Bathe a Boa.* Carolrhoda, 1986. A child struggles to get his reluctant pet boa into the tub.

McPhail, David. *Andrew's Bath.* Little Brown, 1984. Andrew's first all-by-himself bath is an adventuresome experience.

Matsuoka, Kymomko. *There's a Hippo in My Bath.* Doubleday, 1989. A turtle, two penguins, a hippopotamus, and other animals join a boy for fun in the bathtub.

Ray, Mary Lyn. *Mud.* Harcourt Brace, 1996. As the winter snow melts, the earth turns into squishy, glorious mud.

Roffey, Maureen. *Bathtime.* Four Winds, 1989. Two dirty children enjoy the adventure of getting clean in a bath and getting ready for bed. *Note: Makes a good flannel board story.*

Thompson, Sue. *In My Bathroom.* Delacorte, 1990. A young pig describes his activities in the bathroom while preparing for bed.

Watanabe, Shigeo. *I Can Take a Bath.* Philomel, 1987. A baby bear does not want to take a bath until his father joins him in the tub.

Wash Your Face and Hands

Wash your face and hands each day,
(pretend to wash)
Wash them just this way,
You will be clean,
You will look keen,
So wash them each day!
[Action Rhyme]

Bath!

(To the tune of "Mulberry Bush.")

This is the way we fill the bath,
fill the bath, fill the bath.
This is the way we fill the bath,
so early in the morning.

Repeat with: "Wash ourselves," "Scrub our face," "Wash our hair."
[Song]

Flannel board bath fun

Create your own flannel board similar to the song "The Twelve Days of Christmas." Begin with a bathtub and add things such as "one rubber duck, two bars of soap," etc., using the tune from the Christmas song.
[Song]

Bath Time

(Follow actions "drying" self as indicated.)

After a bath I try, try, try,
To rub myself dry, dry, dry.
Hands to dry, fingers and toes.
Two wet legs and a shiny nose.
Just think how much less time it would take,
If I were a dog and could shake, shake, shake!
[Action Rhyme]

☀ **Story Souvenir:** Sponges
Use a scissors or die cut machine to cut sponges into hearts, circles, etc.

Be My Valentine

Damon, Lavra. *Secret Valentine*. Troll, 1988. Molly the mouse tries to find out who sent her an anonymous Valentine.

Ehrlich, Fred. *A Valentine for Mrs. Vanilla*. Viking, 1991. All the kid's in Ms. Vanilla's class make Valentines for the party, including a very special one for their teacher.

Flack, Marjorie. *Ask Mr. Bear*. Macmillan, 1971. A young boy searches, with the help of his animal friends, for the perfect present for his mother. *Note: Makes a good flannel board story.*

Greydanus, Rose. *Valentine's Day Grump*. Troll, 1981. While a Valentine might make Gus happy, nobody dares give him one.

Morris, Anne. *Loving*. Lothrop, 1990. Color photographs provide examples of the many ways love is expressed.

Whitehead, Pat. *The Best Valentine Book*. Troll, 1985. While Big Benny is blue because he doesn't receive any Valentines, the reader meets the letters of the alphabet.

My Valentine

My Valentine is red,
My Valentine is blue.
I drop it in the mailbox,
And send it off to you!
[Rhyme]

Love to You

(To the tune of "Skip To My Lou.")

Love, love, love to you,
Love, love, love to you,
Love, love, love to you,
Love to you my darling.
I love being with you, yes I do,
I love being with you, yes I do,
I love being with you, yes I do,
Love to you my darling.
[Song]

Counting Valentines

Here's a valentine,
And here's a valentine
(make heart shapes with fingers)
A great big valentine I see.
(arch arms over head to form a giant heart)
Are you ready?
Can we count them?
One, two, three!
(hold up one, two, and three fingers)
[Action Rhyme]

Music: "Skidamarink" from ***Wee Sing*** by Pam Beall. Price Stern Sloan, 1984.

☼ **Story Souvenir:** <u>Valentines</u>
Put out red paper hearts, crayons, and stickers, then let the adults help the children decorate.

Bears

Arnosky, Jim. *Every Autumn Comes the Bear.* Putnam, 1993. Every autumn, a bear appears in a field behind a farm and goes through a set of rituals before finding a place to hibernate.

Barton, Byron, *The Three Bears.* HarperCollins, 1991. The traditional tale is illustrated with bright, colorful, simple pictures.

Bird, E.J. *How Do Bears Sleep?* Carolrhoda, 1990. This book describes in verse what goes on in a bear's den during hibernation.

Dabcovich, Lydia. *Sleepy Bear.* Dutton, 1982. Bear gets ready for both his hibernation and his springtime awakening.

Degen, Bruce. *Teddy Bear Towers.* HarperCollins, 1991. A boy pretends to be king of an imaginary land of teddy bears and tries to keep his younger brother out.

Kozikowski, Renate. *The Teddy Bear's Picnic.* Aladdin, 1990. Presents the text of the familiar song about the festivities at the teddy bear's picnic.

Richardson, John. *Ten Bears in a Bed.* Hyperion, 1992. These moveable, pop-up illustrations show ten bears, nine of which fall out of bed when the little one says, "Roll over."

Rylands, Ljiljana. *Teddy Bear's Friend.* Dutton, 1989. Teddy bear is looking for one special friend through peek-a-boo, die-cut pages.

Theobalds, Prue. *Ten Tired Teddies.* Peter Bedrick, 1992. Count the bears as they prepare for tea, bath, storytime, and bed.

Yekati, Nicki. *Hi, Bears, Bye, Bears!* Orchard, 1991. A child chooses from among a group of lively teddy bears.

Young, Ruth. *Golden Bear.* Viking, 1992. Golden Bear and his human companion do things such as play the violin, talk to a bug, and dream together.

A Bear Eats Honey

A bear eats honey. *(pretend to eat)*
He thinks it's yummy
In his tummy. *(rub tummy)*
But the bees don't think it's funny. *BUZZZZZZ!*
[Action Rhyme]

The Bear

Here is the cave, *(bend fingers on one hand)*
Inside is a bear, *(put thumb inside fingers)*
Now he comes out,
To get some fresh air. *(pop out thumb)*
[Fingerplay]

Little Brown Bear

(To the tune of "Little Brown Jug.")

In the woods, in your den,
Or are you out to hunt again?
Use your teeth, use your claws,
Eat some honey with your paws.
Chorus: Ha ha, ha, hee, hee, hee,
Little brown bear, where can you be?
Ha ha, ha, hee, hee, hee,
Little brown bear, where can you be?
In the woods or in your cave,
How does a little bear behave?
On the bed or in a chair,
You are just a teddy bear.

Repeat chorus.
[Song]

☼ **Story Souvenir:** Bear stick puppet
Photocopy the bear pattern onto brown paper and cut out. Tape to a craft stick.

Birds

Ehlert, Lois. *Feathers for Lunch*. Harcourt Brace Jovanovich, 1990. A cat encounters twelve birds, but can't catch even one, so ends up with only feathers to eat.

Hirschi, Ron. *What is a Bird?* Walker, 1991. Text and color photographs describe the basic characteristics of birds.

Mainwarning, Jane. *My Feather.* Doubleday, 1990. This book uses very simple feather activities to introduce basic science concepts.

Nodset, Joan. *Who Took the Farmer's Hat?* HarperCollins, 1962. Farmer looks all over for his hat, but finds only various round, brown objects.

Ward, Helen. *Beautiful Birds.* Bell Books, 1991. Ten boldly illustrated birds are accompanied by simple poetic narratives about them.

Wolff, Ashley. *A Year of Birds.* Dodd Mead, 1984. Ellie's country home is visited by many beautiful birds throughout the year.

Five Birds

Five birds up in a tree,
A father, a mother, and little birds three.
(hold up five fingers)
One ate a bug,
One ate a worm,
One just sat and waited his turn.
(hold up one, two, and three fingers)
[Fingerplay]

Two Little Black Birds

Chorus
Two little black birds sitting on a hill
(point index fingers up)
One named Jack, *(move one hand forward)*
And the other named Jill.
(move the other hand forward)

Fly away, Jack,
(move one hand behind your back)
Fly away Jill.
(move the other hand behind your back)
Come back, Jack,
(return hand to the front)
Come back, Jill.
(move the other hand to the front)

Repeat chorus.
[Song]

Little Bird

I saw a little bird go hop, hop, hop. *(hop)*
I told the little bird to stop, stop, stop.
(hold up hand, palm out)
I went to the window to say
   "How do you do?" *(bow)*
He wagged his little tail and away he flew.
(make flying motion with arms)
[Action Rhyme]

☼ **Story Souvenir:** Baby bird puppet
Photocopy the bird pattern onto colored paper. Cut out and tape to a craft stick.

Birthdays

Stories to Read ABC 123

Argent, Kerry. ***Happy Birthday, Wombat!*** Joy Street, 1991. Various Australian animals try to surprise wombat on his birthday in this lift-the-flap story.

Asch, Frank. ***Happy Birthday, Moon.*** Simon & Schuster, 1988. Bear buys a birthday present for his friend, the moon.

Bornstein, Ruth. ***Little Gorilla.*** Seabury, 1976. Everybody in the jungle loves Little Gorilla, even after he grows up.

Butterworth, Nick. ***Just Like Jasper!*** Little Brown, 1989. Jasper the cat chooses a birthday present that looks just like he does.

Hill, Eric. ***Spot's Birthday Party.*** Putnam, 1982. Spot gets a surprise party in this lift-the-flap book.

Yolen, Jane. ***Mouse's Birthday.*** Putnam, 1993. One by one, the creatures on the farm try to squeeze into mouse's tiny house to help him celebrate his birthday.

Make a Wish

Big chocolate cake,
(make circle with arms)
Ice cream in a dish.
(cup hands)
Here are the candles,
(wiggle fingers)
Now make a wish!
blow on fingers and make into fists)
[Action Rhyme]

Birthday Cake

(Make the motions the words suggest.)
Today is my birthday,
Let's make a birthday cake.
Mix and stir,
Stir and mix,
Then into the oven to bake.
Peek in the oven,
See how it bakes.
Sniff, sniff, it smells so good,
My beautiful birthday cake!
[Action Rhyme]

Song: "Happy Birthday to You" from ***Happy Birthday*** by Sharon, Lois, and Bram. Elephant Records, 1988.

☼ **Story Souvenir:** Birthday cake coloring sheet. Let the kids draw the birthday candles and color the cake. Pattern on the next page.

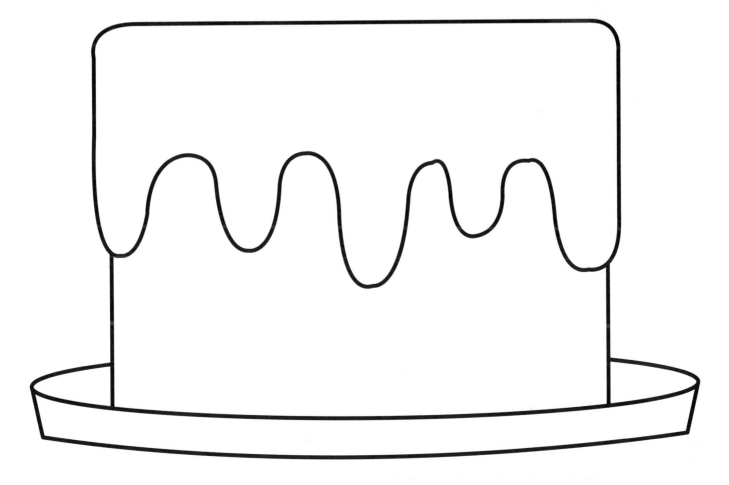

Boats

Allen, Pamela. *Who Sank the Boat?* Coward McCann, 1990. Various animals go on a boat ride and end up in the water.

Burningham, John. *Mr. Gumpy's Outing.* Holt, 1970. Mr. Gumpy takes his boat out with two children and a load of animals with very wet results.

Davies, Kay. *My Boat.* Gareth Stevens, 1990. This simple science book shows boat facts and very easy boat activities.

Schecter, Ben. *If I Had a Ship.* Doubleday, 1970. Although a young boy imagines the travels he would take on a ship, he always returns home to his mother.

Shaw, Nancy. *Sheep on a Ship.* Houghton Mifflin, 1989. The same sheep from the book *Sheep in a Jeep* go on a sea voyage and run into a storm.

Meet the Boats

Toot, toot, toot,
(pretend to pull whistle)
Chug, chug, chug,
I'm a tugboat!
Row, row, row,
(pretend to row)
To and fro,
I'm a rowboat!
Swish, swish, swish,
(raise arms over head and sway)
Blow, blow, blow,
I'm a sailboat!
Whee, whee, wheee,
(Put hands together in a cone shape and move forward.)
I'm fast you see,
I'm a speed boat!
[Action Rhyme]

Soap Boat and Other Floaties

Bring a bar of Ivory soap, a sponge, ping-pong ball, and a twig to your toddler session. Also bring a dishpan or tub filled with water, a pair of scissors, a plastic straw, a small triangle of construction paper and tape. Construct an Ivory soap boat using the soap, straw, construction paper, and tape. Use the scissors to dig a hole in the soap and place the straw "flagpole" in the hole. Tape the triangle on for a "sail." Float the Ivory soap boat, and let the children experiment with the other floating objects.

The Boat on the Waves

(To the tune of "The Wheels on the Bus.")

The boat on the waves goes rock, rock, rock,
Rock, rock, rock,
Rock, rock, rock.
The boat on the waves goes rock, rock, rock,
All around the lake.

Repeat with "The wind in the sail goes swish, swish, swish"; "The waves on the lake go splish, splash, splash"; etc.

[Song]

☼ **Story Souvenir:** Sailboat puppet
Photocopy onto blue paper. Cut out and tape to a craft stick.

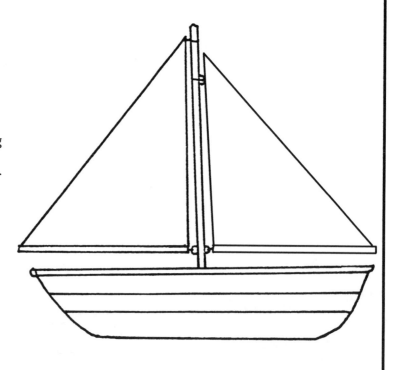

Bugs, Bugs, Bugs

Stories to Read ABC 123

Bunting, Eve. *Flower Garden.* Harcourt Brace Jovanovich, 1994. Helped by her father, a young girl prepares a flower garden as a present for her mother.

Carle, Eric. *The Very Busy Spider.* Philomel, 1984. Several farm animals try to stop a spider from her work, but she persists and ends up with a beautiful and functional web.

Fleming, Denise. *In the Tall, Tall Grass.* Holt, 1991. Rhymed text presents a child's eye view of the creatures found in the grass all through the day.

Fowler, R. *Ladybug on the Move.* Doubleday, 1994. Ladybug searches for a home through die-cut pages. Features a removable cardboard ladybug.

Lacome, Julie. *Garden.* Candlewick, 1993. Creatures found in a garden are animated by the reader by placing fingers through die-cut holes in the pages.

Oppenheim, Joanne. *You Can't Catch Me!* Houghton Mifflin, 1986. A pesky black fly taunts all the animals until it meets a turtle.

Soya, Kiyoshi. *House of Leaves.* Doubleday, 1987. Sarah shares her temporary rain shelter with several garden creatures.

Trapini, Ida. *The Itsy Bitsy Spider.* Whispering Coyote, 1993. The traditional song is illustrated with charming pictures and several expanded verses.

Five Little Ants

Five little ants in an ant hill, *(close fist, palm down)*
Busily working and never still. *(wiggle knuckles)*
Do you think that they are alive?
See them come out—
One, two, three, four, five.
(raise fingers one at a time)
[Fingerplay]

Ladybug

I saw a ladybug fly through the air;
But when I tried to catch her, she wasn't there.
She was so pretty, red and black—
I waved goodbye as she flew back.
(Wave)
[Action Rhyme]

Fuzzy Wuzzy Caterpillar

Fuzzy wuzzy caterpillar,
Into a corner will creep.
(creep fingers)
He'll spin himself a blanket,
And then fall fast asleep.
(rest head on hands and close eyes)
Fuzzy wuzzy caterpillar,
Very soon will rise.
(awaken)
And find he has grown lovely wings—
Now he's a butterfly!
(raise arms up from sides)
[Action Rhyme]

Busy Spider

(To the tune of "Farmer in the Dell")

The spider spins her web.
The spider spins her web.
She works all day,
Can't stop and play.
The spider spins her web.
The spider catches a fly.
The spider catches a fly.
She caught her lunch,
Now it's time to munch.
The spider catches a fly.
[Song]

☺ **Story Souvenir:** Ladybug finger puppet
Photocopy the ladybug pattern onto red paper. Cut out and tape to a child's finger with tape.

Cats and Kittens

Stories to Read ABC 123

Astley, Judy. ***When One Cat Woke Up.*** Dial, 1990. A cat wrecks the house in this numerical romp.

Bernhard, Durga. ***What's Maggie Up To?*** Henry Holt, 1992. The dwellers in an apartment wonder what has become of a wandering cat.

Hirschi, Ron. ***What Is a Cat?*** Walker, 1991. Text and color photographs describe the basic characteristics of cats.

James, Betsy. ***He Wakes Me.*** Orchard, 1991. A girl describes her interactions with her cat, from waking in the morning to going to bed at night.

Lehman, Jeff. ***Sleepy Kittens.*** Tambourine, 1993. These kittens manage to sleep everywhere except their special bed.

Oppenheim, Joanne. ***Do You Like Cats?*** Bantam, 1993. Rhymed text presents cats and cat behavior.

Pryor, Ainslie. ***The Baby Blue Cat and a Whole Batch of Cookies.*** Viking, 1989. Baby Blue Cat can't resist sneaking in the kitchen and eating all of the cookies his mother has made.

Simon, Norma. ***Where Does My Cat Sleep?*** Whitman, 1982. All the members of the family sleep in their own beds, except for Rocky the cat, who sleeps wherever he pleases.

Five Little Kittens

One, two, three, four, five.
(Hold up fingers and count them.)
Five little kittens standing in a row.
They nod their heads to the children just so.
(bend fingers)
They run to the left, *(wiggle fingers left)*
They run to the right, *(wiggle fingers right)*
They stand and stretch in the bright sunlight.
(stretch fingers wide)
[Fingerplay]

Two Little Kittens

Two little kittens found a ball of yarn,
(cup hands together to form a ball)
As they were playing in the barn.
(bring hands together over head to form a roof)
One little kitten jumped in the hay,
(jump)
The other little kitten ran away.
(run in place)
[Action Rhyme]

I'm a Little Kitten

(To the tune of "I'm a Little Teapot.")
I'm a little kitten, soft and furry.
I will be your friend so don't you worry.
Right up on your lap, I like to hop.
I purr, purr, purr and never stop.
[Song]

☼ **Story Souvenir:** Cat nametag
Photocopy the cat pattern onto colored paper and cut out. Punch a hole in the top and thread on yarn to make into a nametag or necklace.

Clothing

Alborough, Jez. *Clothesline.* Candlewick, 1993. The animals have all hung out their clothes to dry on the clothesline. The reader can guess, by lifting flaps, which clothes belong to each one.

Brett, Jan. *The Mitten.* Putnam, 1989. Several animals sleep in a mitten until bear sneezes. *Note: Bring a real mitten to show when sharing story.*

Campbell, Rod. *Buster Keeps Warm.* Barrons, 1988. A little boy puts on warm clothes for his winter play.

Dudko, Mary Ann. *Barney's Hats.* Lyons Group, 1993. Barney the dinosaur is photographed wearing hats from various occupations.

London, Jonathan. *Froggy Gets Dressed.* Puffin, 1996. Froggy wants to play in the snow, but keeps getting called in by his mom for more clothes.

Miller, Bruce. *Whose Shoe?* Greenwillow, 1991. This book illustrates footwear with color photographs and matches each shoe to the appropriate wearer.

Morris, Anne. *Hats, Hats, Hats.* Mulberry, 1989. Color photographs introduce hats of all kinds.

VanLaan, Nancy. *This Is the Hat.* Little Brown, 1992. Cumulative verses follow an old man's hat as it becomes home to several animals before returning home to it's rightful owner.

Watanabe, Sheigo. *How Do I Put It On?* Philomel, 1979. A baby bear demonstrates the right and wrong way to dress. *Note: Use a teddy bear and baby clothes to demonstrate as you read the story.*

J-E-A-N-S

(To the tune of "BINGO.")

Of all the clothes I like to wear
My favorite are my blue jeans,
J-E-A-N-S
J-E-A-N-S
J-E-A-N-S
Don't you like them too?

Repeat the verse, eliminatingone letter of JEANS on each round and replacing it with a hand clap. Continue until you have replaced the whole word with clapping.
[Song]

Look at Me

Look at me! *(point to self)*
Upon my head is a hat of red. *(place hands on head)*
And I have new shoes upon my feet. *(point to feet)*
Look at me!
Hip-hip-hooray!
With a shirt and pants, *(point to each)*
I'm ready to play.
[Action Rhyme]

My Zipper Suit

My zipper suit is bunny brown
The top zips up, *(pretend to zip)*
The legs zip down. *(pretend to zip)*
Zip it up,
Zip it down.
I like to wear it on the town!
[Action Rhyme]

Ten Little Clothespins

(Use the clothespin pattern to create flannel board pieces for this rhyme)

Ten little clothespins hanging on a line.
One lost his grip and then there were nine.
One broke his spring and then there were eight.
Eight little clothespins in a line so even,
One went snip-snap and then there were seven.
Seven little clothespins holding up a slip,
One jumped off and then there were six.
Six little clothespins—are you keeping score?
Two took flip-flops and then there were four.
Four little clothespins straight as can be,
One opened his mouth and then there were three.
Three little clothespins, holding something blue,
One turned a somersault and then there were two.
Two little clothespins looking at the sun,
One felt a raindrop and then there was one.
One little clothespin left alone to say,
"It's the end of the line—see you next washday!"
[Fingerplay]

Color

Baker, Alan. *White Rabbit's Color Book.* Kingfisher, 1994. White rabbit jumps from one color bowl to the next, changing colors until he ends up brown.

Ehlert, Lois. *Planting a Rainbow.* Harcourt Brace Jovanovich, 1988. A mother and child plant a rainbow of colors in the family garden.

Emberley, Ed. *Go Away, Big Green Monster.* Little Brown, 1992. Die-cut pages reveal bits of a monster in a story that will help with nighttime fears.

Martin, Bill. *Brown Bear, Brown Bear, What Do You See?* Henry Holt, 1983. Children see a variety of colored animals.

Rosetti, Christina. *Color.* HarperCollins, 1992. An introduction to colors through a simple, classic poem.

Serfozo, Mary. *Who Said Red?* Margaret K. McElderry, 1988. A rhyming introduction to colors with an emphasis on red.

Color

Blue is the lake,
(point to floor)
Yellow is the sun,
(point to sky)
Silver are the stars,
When the day is done.
(wiggle fingers in the air)
Red is the apple,
(make small circle with hands)
Green is a tree,
(raise arms over head like branches)
Brown is a chocolate cookie for me. *YUM!*
(rub tummy)
[Action Rhyme]

Color Table

Bring a small table or tray, an assortment of objects that are the same color, and a napkin or cloth of the same color to the session. Start off with the bright primary colors (red, yellow, and blue). Place the objects around the room where they can easily be found. Cover the table or tray with the colored cloth. Invite the children and their adult to explore the area and place anything that is the color of the cloth on the tray.

Pink

My favorite color is pink, I think,
(shrug shoulders)
But red is pretty, too.
It's one or the other unless I discover,
(hold out one hand then the other)
I'm suddenly partial to blue!
[Action Rhyme]

☼ **Story Souvenir:** <u>Colors coloring sheet</u>:
Photocopy the coloring chart on the next page for children to complete.

I Can Name These Colors

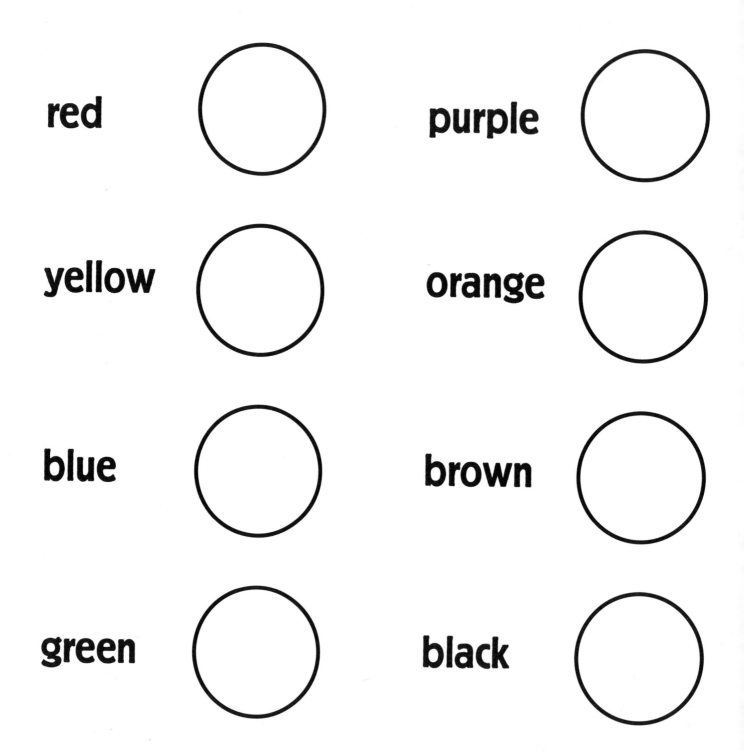

red

purple

yellow

orange

blue

brown

green

black

Dog Dreams

Evans, Nancy. *Hunky Dory Ate It*. Dutton, 1992. Hunky Dory eats everything, including medicine from the vet.

———. *Hunky Dory Found It*. Houghton Mifflin, 1994. Hunky Dory takes pieces of clothing and objects from everyone he meets, but eventually gives them back in the end.

Harper, Isabelle. *My Dog Rosie*. Blue Sky Press, 1994. While her grandfather works in his studio, a very young girl takes care of the family dog.

Hill, Eric. **Spot books.** Putnam, 1982 and later. A series of lift-the-flap books, board and other books about a very cute puppy.

Kopper, Lisa. *Daisy is a Mommy*. Dutton, 1987. Daisy is a funny mommy to three cute puppies.

Leslie, Amanda. *Play, Puppy, Play.* Candlewick, 1993. Die-cut holes in the illustrations allow the reader to animate animals such as a dog, cat, caterpillar, snail, and others with their fingers. (I)

Mott, Evelyn. *Hot Dog.* Random House, 1997. Rhythmic text and full-color photographs of dogs set against computer-generated backgrounds make this introductory text fun. (I)

Robart, Rose. *The Cake That Mack Ate.* Atlantic Monthly, 1987. A cumulative tale about a dog and a birthday cake.

Sharrat, Nick. *Monday, Run Day.* Candlewick, 1992. Very simple rhymed text follows a dog's weekly activities.

Trapini, Ida. *Oh, Where, Oh, Where Has My Little Dog Gone?* Whispering Coyote, 1995. The traditional song has the little dog exploring far and wide before returning home.

My Little Puppy

I have a little puppy,
Her fur is black and gray.
One day I tried to bathe her,
To wash the dirt away.
I washed my little puppy,
Then dried her with a towel.
She seemed to really like her bath—
She didn't even growl.
[Rhyme]

Five Little Puppies

(Use the puppy pattern provided to create flannel board pieces for this rhyme.)

Five little puppies were playing in the sun.
This one saw a rabbit and he began to run.
This one saw a butterfly and he began to race.
This one saw a kitty cat and he began to chase.
This one tried to catch his tail and
he went round and round.
This one was so quiet he never made a sound.
(point to and bend down each finger in succession)
[Fingerplay]

☼ **Story Souvenir:** Puppy nametag
Photocopy the puppy pattern onto colored paper and cut out. Punch a hole in the top. Run a piece of yarn through the hole to make a puppy nametag or necklace.

Puppies
(To the tune of "Ten Little Indians.")

One little, two little, three little puppies,
Lying in a pile, all sleepy and lumpy.
Four little, five little, six little puppies,
Lying in a pile, all sleepy and lumpy.
Seven little, eight little, nine little puppies,
Ten little puppies in a pile.
[Song]

Elephants

Stories to Read ABC 123

Ets, Marie Hall. *Elephant in a Well*. Viking, ND. The traditional tale of the animals who try to help the elephant by pulling him out of the well.

Kasza, Keiko. *When the Elephant Walks*. Putnam, 1990. When the elephant walks, he sets off an animal chain reaction in this neverending tale.

Leydenfrost, Robert. *Ten Little Elephants*. Doubleday, 1975. Ten elephants have all kinds of active adventures until only one is left. *Note: Makes a good flannel board story.*

McKee, David. *Elmer, the Patchwork Elephant*. Lothrop, 1968. Elmer is an elephant, but he is not gray, he is patchwork.

Riddell, Chris. *The Trouble With Elephants*. Harper Trophy, 1988. Despite all the trouble an elephant cane be, a young girl explains that you can't help but love them.

Sheppard, Jeff. *The Right Number of Elephants*. Harper & Row, 1990. A counting book in which a little girl relies on the help of her elephant friends.

The Elephant

An elephant goes like this and that,
(sway body left to right)
He's terribly big and terribly fat.
(raise arms out from sides to show fatness)
He has no fingers,
(wiggle fingers)
He has no toes,
(point to toes)
But goodness gracious what a nose!
(hold arm in front of face like trunk)
[Action Rhyme]

Five Elephants

One elephant went out to play,
On a spider's web one day.
He had such enormous fun,
He asked another elephant to come.

*(Hold up 1, 2 3, 4, 5, fingers.
Repeat verses with 2, 3, 4, 5)*

Five elephants went out to play,
All on a spider's web one day.
They had such enormous fun,
They didn't ask another elephant to come!
[Fingerplay]

Elephant

(To the tune of "Row, Row, Row Your Boat.")

Go, go, go, so slow,
Make a thunder sound!
See his trunk, so long and thick,
The elephant's in town!
[Song]

☼ **Story Souvenir:** Elmer coloring sheet
Photocopy the pattern on the next page and have children color Elmer, the patchwork elephant.

Fall Is Here!

Arnosky, Jim. *Every Autumn Comes the Bear.* Putnam, 1993. Every autumn, a bear appears in a field behind a farm and goes through certain rituals before finding a place to hibernate.

Ehlert, Lois. *Red Leaf, Yellow Leaf.* Harcourt Brace Jovanovich, 1991. A child describes the growth of a maple tree from seed to sapling.

Moncure, Jane. *Fall is Here!* Children's Press, 1975. This book prescribes in verse the various changes and activities associated with fall.

My First Look at the Seasons. Dorling Kindersley, 1990. Labeled color photographs depict some of the highlights of each season.

Neilsen-Barshun, Rochelle. *In Fall.* Children's Press, 1985. A poem describes the various aspects of the fall season.

Schecter, Ben. *When Will the Snow Trees Grow?* HarperCollins, 1993. A boy and a bear celebrate the changes fall brings and the preparations for winter.

Wheeler, Stephanie. *Mamalade's Yellow Leaf.* Knopf, 1982. Marmalade the orange cat chases a yellow leaf. *Note: Use real or paper yellow leaves to tell this story.*

Fall

Autumn winds begin to blow,
(blow)
Colored leaves fall fast and slow.
(wiggle fingers down fast and slow)
Twirling, whirling all around.
(turn around)
Until at last they touch the ground.
(touch ground)
[Action Rhyme]

Autumn Time

The trees are gently dropping,
Leaves onto the ground.
(flutter fingers down)
The flowers are all nodding,
Down and all around.
(turn around slowly)
The wind is blowing,
A chilly breeze.
(sway back and forth)
The birds are flying,
Into the trees.
(flap arms like wings)
[Action Rhyme]

Leaves

(To the tune of "Row, Row, Row Your Boat.")
I like to make a pile of leaves,
And jump and tumble around.
I like to hear them as I walk,
They make a crunchy sound.
[Song]

☼ **Story Souvenir:** <u>Fall tree</u>
Photocopy the tree pattern on the next page and let the children use crayons in fall colors to draw leaves.

Fire!

Stories to Read **ABC** **123**

Bridwell, Norman. ***Clifford the Fire House Dog.*** Scholastic Inc., 1994. Clifford visits his cousin in the city, who is a fire house dog.

The Great Big Fire Engine Book. Golden Book, 1950. This classic book with large illustrations shows how firemen respond to a fire.

Mayer, Mercer. ***Fireman Critter.*** Simon & Schuster, 1986. A little critter pretends to be a fire fighter, causing his family all kinds of problems.

Paterson, Bettina. ***Who's at the Firehouse?*** Putnam, 1996. Lift the sturdy flaps on this book and see who is hiding at the fire house. (I)

Rey, H.A. ***Curious George Visits a Fire Station.*** Houghton Mifflin, 1985. Curious George sets off a false fire alarm, but redeems himself by rescuing a dalmatian puppy.

Rockwell, Anne. ***Fire Engines.*** Dutton, 1986. This book describes fire engines and how fire fighters put out fires.

Smoky
(To the tune of "BINGO.")

There was a fireman had a dog and
Smoky was her name-Oh!
S-M-O-K-Y, S-M-O-K-Y, S-M-O-K-Y,
And Smoky was her name-Oh!
(Repeat the verse, eliminating one letter of SMOKY on each round and replacing it with a hand clap. Continue until you have replaced the whole word with clapping.)
[Song]

Stop, Drop, and Roll

Clothes on fire?
Don't get scared!
Stop, drop, and roll!
(do actions)
[Action Rhyme]

Firefighter
(To the tune of "I'm a Little Teapot.")

I'm a fire fighter in a big red truck,
I bring out the hoses and put the ladder up.
I put out the fires and I'm your friend.
I'm the fire fighter and it's the end.
[Song]

The Firefighter

This fire fighter rings the bell,
This fire fighter holds the hose so well.
This fire fighter slides down a pole,
This fire fighter chops a hole.
This fire fighter climbs higher and higher,
And all the fire fighters put out the fire.
(hold up each finger beginning with thumb)
[Fingerplay]

☼ **Story Souvenir:** Fire Safety Award
Photocopy, enlarge, and personalize the awards.

I'm Fire Smart

Fire Safety Oath

I, _____
Your Name

promise to practice fire safety

rules and do everything I can to

prevent fires.

Foxes

Arnosky, Jim. *Watching Foxes.* Lothrop, 1985. Four baby foxes play near their den.

Fox, Mem. *Hattie and the Fox.* Bradbury, 1986. Hattie, a black hen, discovers a fox in the bushes and gets a range of reactions from the other farm animals.

Giffard, Hannah. *Red Fox.* Dial, 1991. Red fox searches for food for himself and his mate, then returns home to find a new family awaits him.

Hogrogian, Nonny. *One Fine Day.* Macmillan, 1971. In this Caldecott Award-winning book, a fox loses his tail when he drinks a pail of milk that does not belong to him.

Hutchins, Pat. *Rosie's Walk.* Simon & Schuster, 1968. Although unaware that a fox is following her, Rosie the hen still manages to lead him from one accident to another.

Walsh, Ellen. *You Silly Goose.* Harcourt Brace Jovanovich, 1992. A silly goose is convinced that a mouse is a fox until the real fox comes along to set her straight.

This Little Fox

This little fox went to the forest, *(wiggle thumb)*
This little fox stayed home. *(wiggle index finger)*
This little fox ate berries, *(wiggle third finger)*
This little fox ate none. *(wiggle ring finger)*
And this little fox went *(wiggle pinky finger)*
Swish, swish, swish his tail *(swish hand back and forth)*
All the way home!
(make fist and hide hand behind back)
[Fingerplay]

Fox Song

(To the tune of "Ten Little Indians.")

One little, two little, three little foxes,
Four little, five little, six little foxes,
Seven little, eight little, nine little foxes,
Ten foxes in their den!
[Song]

Foxes in Their Den

1, 2, 3, 4, 5, in a row,
The foxes in their den.
Sitting right beside them
Are 6, 7, 8, 9, and 10.
(hold up fingers one at a time)
[Fingerplay]

☀ **Story Souvenir:** <u>Fox sack puppet</u>
Photocopy and enlarge the fox pattern onto light brown or orange-red paper and cut out. Paste the fox head to the flat bottom of a lunch sack to create a puppet.

Frogs & Turtles

Asch, Frank. *Turtle Tale*. Dial, 1978. A turtle has some surprises when he sticks his head out of his shell.

Faulkner, Matt. *Wide Mouth Frog*. Dial, 1996. A wide mouth frog is very curious about what other animals eat until she meets a crocodile that eats frogs. A moveable, pop-up book.

Florian, Douglas. *Turtle Day*. Crowell, 1989. Turtle's adventures include sunning himself, swimming and being frightened by a snake.

Jonas, Anne. *Splash!* Greenwillow, 1995. A young girl's pets jump in and out of the water, changing the answer to the question "How many are in the pond?"

Kalan, Robert. *Jump, Frog, Jump!* Greenwillow, 1991. A cumulative tale in which a turtle, who is after a fly, tries to avoid being captured himself. *Note: Makes a good flannel board story.*

Leditschke, Anna. *Tiny Timothy Turtle*. Gareth Stevens, 1991. A very small turtle finds some advantages to being tiny, although he eventually grows up to be very large.

Turner, Charles. *The Turtle and the Moon*. Dutton, 1991. A young turtle is lonely until he makes friends with the moon.

Jump, Jump

Jump, jump went the little green frog one day,
Jump, jump went the little green frog.
Jump, jump went the little green frog one day,
An his eyes went blink, blink, blink.
Blink, blink went the little green frog one day,
Blink, blink went the little green frog.
Blink, blink went the little green frog one day,
An his tongue went glup, glup, glup.
Glup, glup went the little green frog one day,
Glup, glup went the little green frog.
Glup, glup went the little green frog one day,
And his legs went jump, jump, jump.
[Song]

Little Turtle

(Use the pattern to make a turtle finger puppet)

I had a little turtle, *(make a fist)*
He lived in a box. *(put hand over fist)*
He swam in the water, *(make swimming motion)*
And he climbed on the rocks.
(make one hand climb up the other arm)
He snapped at a mosquito,
He snapped at a flea,
He snapped at a minnow,
And he snapped at me!
(clap on the word "snap")
He caught the mosquito,
He caught the flea,
He caught the minnow,
But he didn't catch me!
(make grabbing motion on the word "caught")
[Action Rhyme]

Listen to the Frog

Listen to the frog,
(cup hand to ear)
Croaking on a log.
It sounds so clear,
For us to hear—Ribbett, ribbett, ribbett.
But what about the other,
Who seems like a brother?
(shrug shoulders)
The turtle crawls around,
But doesn't make a sound—Shhhh.
[Action Rhyme]

Little Turtle

☼ **Story Souvenir:** <u>Frog sack puppet</u>
Photocopy the frog pattern on green paper and cut out. Paste the
frog head to the flat bottom of a lunch sack to create a puppet.
Trace the tongue onto pink paper and cut out. Patse the tongue
under the flap of the head.

Go to Sleep

Alda, Arlene. *Pig, Horse, or Cow, Don't Wake Me Now.* Doubleday, 1994. A peacock's honk sets off a chain reaction of animal sounds as they wake up on a summer morning.

Bang, Molly. *10, 9, 8.* Greenwillow, 1983. The classic, gentle counting lullaby.

Buller, Jon. *I Love You, Good Night.* Simon & Schuster, 1988. A mother and daughter exchange "I love you as much…" phrases at bedtime.

Fox, Mem. *Time for Bed.* Harcourt Brace Jovanovich, 1993. As darkness falls, parents every-where try to get their little ones ready for bed.

Ginsburg, Mirra. *Asleep, Asleep.* Greenwillow, 1992. Everything everywhere is asleep except for the wind and a wakeful child.

Lindbergh, Reeve. *Midnight Farm.* Dial, 1987. The secrets of night on the farm are revealed in a poem.

Moore, Julia. *While You Sleep.* Dutton, 1996. While a baby sleeps, the natural world surrounds the child with continuous activity.

Wheeler, Cindy. *Marmalade's Nap.* Knopf, 1982. Marmalade the orange cat attempts to take a nap.

Bedtime

When bedtime comes I climb the stairs,
I fold my hands and say my prayers.
I climb in bed and turn out the light,
And then I whisper "Goodnight, Goodnight."
[Action Rhyme]

Go to Sleep

Go to sleep now,
Eyes don't peek now,
Dreaming soon you will be,
Very good dreams you will see.
Close your eyes, close them tight,
So you can sleep through the night.
[Rhyme]

Going to Bed

This little child is going to bed, *(point to self)*
Down on the pillow he lays his head.
(rest head on hands)
He wraps himself in a blanket tight. *(hug yourself)*
And this is the way he sleeps all night,
ZZZZZZZZ!
[Action Rhyme]

☺ **Story Souvenir:** Awake/Asleep door hanger
Photocopy and enlarge the door hanger pattern onto heavy paper and cut out both sides. Glue the two sides together and cut out the circle. Use a piece of yarn or ribbon to tie to door knob.

Growing Things

Stories to Read   ABC   123

Bunting, Eve. *Flower Garden.* Harcourt Brace Jovanovich, 1994. Helped by her father, a young girl prepares a flower garden as a surprise for her mother.

Ehlert, Lois. *Growing Vegetable Soup.* Harcourt Brace Jovanovich, 1987. A father and a child grow vegetables and then make soup.

_____. *Planting a Rainbow.* Harcourt Brace Jovanovich, 1988. A mother and child plant a rainbow of flowers in the family garden.

Florian, Douglas. *Vegetable Garden.* Harcourt Brace Jovanovich, 1991. A family plants a vegetable garden and helps it grow to full harvest.

Ford, Miela. *Sunflower.* Greenwillow, 1995. A young girl plants a sunflower seed, waters it, and watches it grow.

Hutchins, Pat. *Titch.* Macmillan, 1971. Little Titch only does small things until the seed he plants grows into a large plant.

Kraus, Ruth. *The Carrot Seed.* Harper & Row, 1945. A boy's family insists that his carrot will not grow, but it does.

McMillan, Bruce. *Counting Wildflowers.* Lothrop, 1986. A counting book with color photographs of flowers illustrating the numbers one through twenty.

Petie, Haris. *The Seed the Squirrel Dropped.* Prentice Hall, 1976. A tiny seed grows into—a cherry pie! *Note: Makes a good flannel board story.*

Here's a Green Leaf

Here's a green leaf, *(show palm)*
And here's a green leaf, *(show other palm)*
That, you see, makes two.
Here is a bud,   *(make a fist)*
That is a flower.
Watch it bloom for you. *(open fingers slowly)*
[Fingerplay]

Planting Time

(To the tune of "Row Your Boat.")

Dig, dig, dig the earth,
Then you plant your seeds.
A gentle rain,
The bright sunshine,
And flowers you will see!
[Song]

Dig a Little Hole

Dig a little hole.
Plant a little seed.
Pour a little water.
Pull a little weed.
Chase a little bug.
There he goes!
Here comes the sun—
Let it grow, grow, grow.
(Do actions as suggested by words.)
[Action Rhyme]

☼ **Story Souvenir:** <u>Sunflower color sheet</u>

Halloween

Benjamin, Allan. *Hallowhat?* Simon & Schuster, 1992. This chubby board book asks rhymed questions about Halloween. *Note: Hallowhat? is very small, but makes a good flannel board story.*

Carter, David. *In a Dark, Dark Wood*. Simon & Schuster, 1991. A old tale about a dark house, wood, etc., with a pop-up surprise at the end.

Freeman, Don. *Corduroy's Halloween*. Viking, 1995. Corduroy visits the pumpkin patch, gets his costume, decorates his house, and then goes trick or treating with his friends.

Roberts, Bethany. *Halloween Mice*. Clarion, 1995. Whirling, skipping mice trick a cat on Halloween.

Sampton, Sheila. *My Haunted House*. Boyd Mills, 1992. A striped cat shows the way through a haunted lift-the-flap mansion.

Ziefert, Harriet. *Scare the Moon*. Candlewick, 1995. A tiny witch and small warlock have a "booing" contest to see which of them can scare the moon.

———. *What is Halloween?* HarperCollins, 1992. Lift the flaps as Little Mouse gets ready for Halloween and trick or treating.

———. *Where is the Halloween Treat?* Puffin, 1985. Lift the flaps and count to see who has the Halloween treats.

Halloween

Here is my pumpkin, round and fat,
(make circle with arms)
Here is a point on a witch's hat.
(make triangle with hands on head)
Here is the mouth of a ghost who says *"BOO!"*
(circle hands around mouth)
And here are owl's eyes, looking at you!
(make circles around eyes with hands)
[Action Rhyme]

Three White Ghosts

(To the tune of "Three Blind Mice." Use pattern for the ghost puppet to create flannel board pieces for this song.)

Three white ghosts,
Three white ghosts,
See how they run,
See how they run,
They all came knocking at my front door,
Collecting candy and treats galore.
I gave them some, but they said "Give me more!"
Those three white ghosts.
[Song]

Halloweeny Spider

(Tune of "The Itsy Bitsy Spider")

The Halloweeny spider,
Crawled in the witch's house,
In came the witch,
And swept the spider out.
Out came the moon,
And she rode off on her broom,
And the Halloweeny spider
Crawled in her house again.
[Song]

Ghost Chant

Ghost so scary,
Ghost so white,
Won't scare me,
On Halloween night!
[Rhyme]

Story Souvenir: <u>Ghost puppet</u>
Photocopy ghost onto white paper and cut out.
Tape to a craft stick.

Hands & Feet

STories to Read **ABC** **123**

Blanchard, Arlene. *Sounds My Feet Make.* Random House, 1988. Pictures and descriptive sound words show the variety of noises two feet can make.

Cauley, Lorinda. *Clap Your Hands.* Putnam, 1992. Rhyming text instructs the listener to perform playful actions with the human and animal characters pictured.

Holzenthaler, Jean. *My Hands Can.* Dutton, 1978. This book describes some of the simple activities hands can do.

Kroll, Virginia. *Hands!* Boyd Mills, 1997. A lively concept book that stimulates the reader to think about hands and all the things they can do.

Parnall, Peter. *Feet!* Collier, 1988. Line drawings present all kinds of feet.

Quinlan, Patricia. *Baby's Feet.* Firefly, 1996. Simple text and pictures show what a baby's feet can do. (I)

————. *Baby's Hands.* Firefly, 1996. Simple text and pictures show what a baby's hands can do. (I)

Let Your Hands

Let your hands go clap, clap, clap.
(clap hands)
Let your feet go tap, tap, tap. *(tap feet)*
Let your head go no, no, no. *(shake head no)*
Shake your hands and fold them so.
(shake hands and fold them in your lap)
[Action Rhyme]

Five Little Fingers

Five little fingers on one hand.
(wiggle fingers)
Two little feet on which to stand.
(point to feet)
Two little hands to hold up high.
(raise hands up)
With them I reach for the sky.
[Action Rhyme]

Wiggle Your Toes

(To the tune of "Row, Row, Row Your Boat.")

Wiggle, wiggle, wiggle your toes,
Wiggle them up and down.
Wiggle them fast,
Wiggle them slow,
Wiggle them all around.
Repeat with wiggle your fingers, clap your hands, stomp your feet.
[Song]

☼ **Story Souvenir:** Hand tracings
Trace pictures of the children's hands and feet for them to color and take home, or have the child make a handprint using washable poster paint or finger paint.

THIS IS MY HAND

Happy Apples

Asch, Frank. *Turtle Tale*. Dial, 1978. Turtle is in for some surprises when he sticks his head out of his shell.

Davies, Kay. *My Apple.* Gareth Stevens, 1990. This simple science book shows facts and very easy apple activities.

Hall, Zoe. *The Apple Pie Tree*. Scholastic Inc., 1996. Shows the life cycle of an apple tree and a family of robins who live in it. Included is a recipe for apple pie.

Pilkey, Dav. *A Friend for Dragon*. Orchard, 1991. Dragon becomes best friends with an apple, mourns it's loss, then rejoices when a whole new tree of apples grow. *Note: Tell the story with an apple and a dragon puppet.*

Ross, Harry. *Fraggle's Alphabet Pie*. Muppet Press, 1988. *The Fraggle Rock* muppets have an A to Z adventure featuring an apple pie.

My Apple

Look at my apple, it's nice and round.
(make ball shape with hands)
It fell from the tree down to the ground.
(make downward motion)
Come share my apple with me, please do.
(make beckoning motion)
My mother will cut it right in two.
(make slicing motion)
Half for me and half for you!
[Fingerplay]

Applesauce
(tune of "Yankee Doodle")

Peel an apple, cut it up,
Cook it in a pot.
When you taste it,
You will find
It's applesauce you've got!
[Song]

Two Red Apples

Way up high,
In a tree, *(raise arms high)*
Two red apples,
Smiled at me! *(smile)*
So I shook the tree,
As hard as I could. *(pretend to shake tree)*
And down fell the apples
Mmmm, they were good! *(rub tummy)*
[Action Rhyme]

Story Souvenir: Apple necklace
Photocopy the apple pattern onto red paper and cut out. Punch a hole in the stem and string on yarn to make a necklace.

Stories to Read ABC 123

Denton, Kady. *The Christmas Boot.* Little Brown, 1990. While playing outside, Jeremy and Alison find a big black boot that is filled with surprises.

Freeman, Don. *Corduroy's Christmas.* Viking, 1992. In this lift-the-flap story, Corduroy wraps gifts, decorates his tree, and goes caroling with friends.

Harrison, Susan. *Christmas With the Bears.* Dutton, 1987. Peek-through pages allow the reader glimpses of a bear family's preparations for Christmas.

Hill, Eric. *Spot's First Christmas.* Price Stern Sloan, 1991. Spot the dog excitedly gets ready for Christmas in this lift-the-flap book.

Moerbeck, Kees. *Oh No, Santa!* Santa chooses several nice trees as a Christmas tree, but each one turns out to be a home of a particular animal.

Morehead, Ruth. *A Christmas Countdown.* Random House, 1992. A rhymed Christmas countdown from ten colored Christmas balls to one Christmas tree.

Whitehead, Pat. *The Christmas Alphabet Book.* Troll, 1985. The letters of the alphabet are shown as Santa leaves late on Christmas Eve.

Ziefert, Harriet. *Nicky's Christmas Surprise.* HarperCollins, 1985. Lift the flaps and help Nicky the cat find the perfect Christmas gift for his mother.

Here is the Chimney

Here is the chimney,
(make a fist and tuck in thumb)
Here is the top
(put other hand over flat top of fist)
Open the lid,
(remove hand)
Out Santa will Pop! *(pop up thumbs)*
[Fingerplay]

Dear Old Santa

(To the tune of "London Bridge.")

Guess whose beard is long and white, long and white, long and white?
Guess whose beard is long and white?
Dear old Santa!

Repeat with "Guess whose boots are shiny and black..."
[Song]

Five Little Bells

(Use the pattern to create flannel board pieces for this rhyme)

Five little bells hanging in a row,
(hold up five fingers)
The first one said, "Ring me slow."
(move thumb slowly)
The second one said, "Ring me fast."
(move index finger quickly)
The third one said "Ring me last."
(move middle finger)
The fourth one said, "I'm like a chime."
(move ring finger)
The fifth one said, "Ring us all at Christmas time."
(wiggle all fingers)
[Fingerplay]

Story Souvenir: <u>Christmas Tree coloring sheet</u>
Photocopy the pattern on the next page for children to color.

Happy Holidays: Christmas tree coloring sheet 53

Stories to Read **ABC** **123**

Daniel, Frank. *Chanukah.* (Fun Shapes Series) Macmillan, 1993. A small board book with die-cut pages featuring Chanukah objects. *Note: This makes a good flannel board story with square shapes.*

DePaola, Tomie. *My First Chanukah.* Putnam, 1989. Introduces, on board pages, some of the objects and activities associated with the celebration of Chanukah.

Kimmel, Eric A. *The Magic Dreidels.* Holiday House, 1996. An old woman swindles Jacob out of his dreidels, but Jacob retrieves them before Hanukkah.

Kimmelman, Leslie. *Hanukkah Lights, Hanukkah Nights.* HarperCollins, 1992. An extended family celebrates the eight nights of Hanukkah.

Five Pieces of Gelt

I have five little pieces of Hanukkah gelt,
The first one said, "Eat me before I melt."
The second one said, "I have gold foil on my side."
The third one said, "Peel me to see where chocolate hides."
The fourth one said, "Eat me fast."
The fifth one said, "I am the last."
(hold up one through five fingers)
[Fingerplay]

Spin, Little Dreidels

Spin, little dreidels, go, go, go. *(spin around)*
Spin, little dreidels, no go slow. *(spin slower)*
Spin, little dreidels, jump so high. *(jump)*
Spin, little dreidels, reach to the sky.
(stretch arms up over head)
Spin, little dreidels, touch your nose. *(touch nose)*
Spin, little dreidels, stand on your toes. *(stand tip-toe)*
Spin, little dreidels, take a hop. *(hop)*
Spin, little dreidels, stop, stop, stop!
[Action Rhyme]

☼ **Story Souvenir:** Menorah coloring sheet

Happy Holidays  Kwanzaa

Chocolate, Deborah. *A Very Special Kwanzaa.* Scholastic Inc., 1986. A simple introduction to the symbols and rituals of Kwanzaa.

Ford, Juwanda. *K Is for Kwanzaa.* Cartwheel, 1997. An alphabet book with facts and beautiful paintings about Kwanzaa.

Grier, Ella. *Seven Days of Kwanzaa.* Viking, 1997.

This book, which has bright pictures bordered by Kente cloth, celebrates Kwanzaa, from lighting candles, to singing songs, to storytelling, and more.

Williams, Nancy. *A Kwanzaa Celebration.* Simon & Schuster, 1995. A bright, bold pop-up book featuring the seven principles of Kwanzaa.

Light a Kinara Candle

Light a kinara candle
See how it glows
Now six are left
All in a row.

Repeat with five, four, three, two, one.
[Fingerplay]

Kwanzaa Today
(To the tune of "Row, Row, Row Your Boat.")

Clap, clap, clap your hands
And sing so merrily
Kwanzaa begins today
We're happy as can be!

Repeat with "stomp your feet," "jump so high," etc.
[Song]

Holiday Candles All in a Row

The first one said "light me, so I will glow."
The second one said, "light me, so I can see."
The third one said, "I'm waiting in line."
The fourth one said, "Light me, I'll really shine."
The fifth one said, "I'll shine so bright."
The sixth one said, "With a beautiful light."
The seventh one said, "My light is strong."
And they burned all night long.

☺ Story Souvenir: <u>Kinara coloring sheet</u>

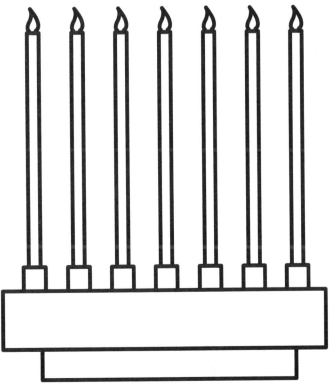

I Love My Daddy

Asch, Frank. *Just Like Daddy.* Simon & Schuster, 1991. Baby Bear does everything just like daddy.

Greenfield, Eloise. *My Daddy and I.* Writers and Readers, 1991. An African American father and son are depicted in this board book.

Hallinan, P. K. *We're Very Good Friends, My Father and I.* Children's Press, 1989. A child explains the mutual activities that create a strong friendship between him and his dad.

McBratney, Sam. *Guess How Much I Love You.* Candlewick Press, 1992. Big Nutbrown Hare and Little Nutbrown Hare play a bedtime "I Love You" game.

McPhail, David. *The Party.* Joy Street, 1990. A boy's stuffed animals come to life and help him have a party to which he has invited his very sleepy father.

Porter-Gaylord, Laurel. *I Love My Daddy Because...* Dutton, 1991. A child explains why he loves his father through pictures of animal father and baby pairs.

Dads Are Best

Teddy bears are nice to clutch,
To hold, to love, to feel, to touch.
(pretend to hug bear)
But daddies are the best of all,
To hug and kiss when you are small.
(hug self)
[Action Rhyme]

Do You Love Me?

(To the tune of "Twinkle, Twinkle Little Star.")

Tell me daddy is it true,
Do you love me like I love you?
Do you love me if I'm bad?
Do you love me if I'm mad?
Yes my darling, I sure do!
Now and always I love you.
[Song]

I Love Daddy

(To the tune of "Frere Jaques.")

I love daddy, I love daddy,
Yes I do, yes I do.
Daddy is my best friend,
Daddy is my best friend.
Mom is too, mom is too.
[Song]

Daddy is My Friend

Daddy is my special friend,
The two of us are close.
(hold up two fingers)
I always like the things we do
And I love him the most!
(hug self)
[Fingerplay]

☀ **Story Souvenir:** Best Dad Award
Photocopy the award pattern and let each child color as a gift for dad.

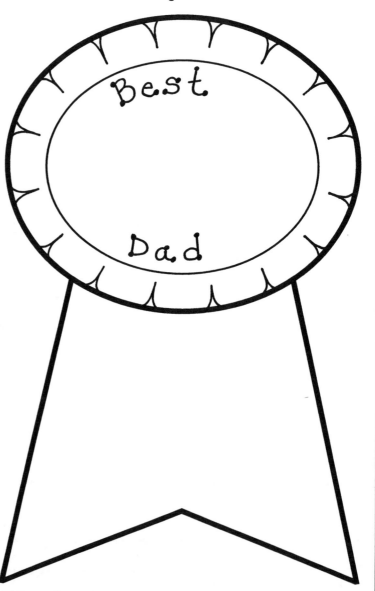

I Love My Mommy

Buller, Jon. *I Love You, Good Night.* Simon & Schuster, 1988. A mother and daughter exchange "I love you as much" phrases at bedtime.

Dijs, Carla. *Are You My Mommy?* Little Simon, 1990. While searching for mom, a baby chick encounters all kinds of animals in pop-up format. (I)

Guarino, Deborah. *Is Your Mama a Llama?* Scholastic Inc., 1989. A young llama asks various animals if their mama is a llama. He finds out in rhyme that their mamas are other animals.

Polushkin, Maria. *Mother, Mother, I Want Another.* Crown, 1978. Mrs. Mouse tries to get baby mouse to sleep by giving him what she thinks he wants. *Note: Makes a good flannel board story.*

Porter-Gaylord, Laurel. *I Love My Mommy Because...* Dutton, 1991. A child explains why he loves his mother through pictures of mother and baby animal pairs.

Stimson, Joan. *Big Panda, Little Panda.* Barron's, 1994. After the arrival of a new baby, Little Panda is now called Big panda, and has some trouble adjusting to the change.

My Family

Here is my pretty mother. *(index finger)*
Here is my father tall. *(middle finger)*
Here is my older brother. *(ring finger)*
Here is the baby, small. *(pinky)*
Who is this person? *(thumb)*
Of course, it's me.
One, two, three, four, five, *(count all fingers)*
Makes a family!
[Fingerplay]

Do You Love Me?
(To the tune of "Twinkle, Twinkle Little Star.")

Tell me mommy is it true
Do you love me like I love you?
Do you love me if I'm bad?
Do you love me if I'm mad?
Yes my darling, I sure do!
Now and always I love you.
[Song]

Mommy

Mommy, mommy
Here are my gifts—
A special hug
And a great big kiss!
[Rhyme]

I Love You
(To the tune of "This Old Man.")

I love you, I love you,
I love you, yes I do.
Oh, yes, oh, yes, oh, y-es I do.
I love you, yes I do.
[Song]

☺ **Story Souvenir:** <u>Mommy portraits</u>
Photocopy the pattern and let each child color a picture of mom as a gift.

Just Ducky

Arnosky, Jim. *All Night Near the Water.* Putnam, 1994. A family of baby ducks stays awake under the care of their mother all night long.

Hammond, Franklin. *Ten Little Ducks.* Douglas and McIntyre, 1987. Ten young ducks complete daily chores and bathing rituals.

Hayes, Sara. *Nine Ducks Nine.* Lothrop, 1990. Mister Fox watches as nine ducks drop out of sight.

Otto, Carolyn. *Ducks, Ducks, Ducks.* HarperCollins, 1991. Four country ducks have an adventure while visiting their city cousin.

Wikler, Linda. *Alfonse, Where Are You?* Crown, 1996. Alfonse the goose cannot find Little Bird when they play hide and seek because he is too noisy.

Yellow Ducky

When a yellow ducky,
Walks down the street,
(walk in place)
Quack! goes his bill,
(open and close hand like duck mouth)
Waddle go his feet.
(waddle in place)
He comes to a puddle and with a bound,
(make circle with one arm)
In goes the ducky and he swims around.
(make other hand jump into circle)
[Action Rhyme]

Quack, Quack

Now I'm up,
(stand)
Now I'm down,
(squat down)
See me waddle all around.
(waddle)
Put my hands behind my back,
Like a duck I'll say, "Quack, quack."
[Action Rhyme]

Five Little Ducks

(Use the duck pattern to make five ducks for telling this as a flannel board story.)

Five little ducks went swimming one day,
Down the pond and far away.
Mother duck said, "Quack, quack, quack."
And four little ducks came swimming back.
(hold up five through zero fingers and repeat with four, three, two, one, none)
Then mother duck said, "Quack, quack, quack!"
(loudly)
And five little ducks came swimming back.
[Fingerplay]

Run, Little Ducks

Run, little ducks, run like a flash, *(run in place)*
Jump in the water with a splash, splash, splash.
(clap three times)
Paddle your feet all around,
(make paddling motion)
Waddle on home when you hear this sound:
(waddle)
Quack, quack, quack!
[Action Rhyme]

☼ **Story Souvenir:** <u>Ducky coloring sheet</u>
Enlarge pattern and give to children to color.

Let's Count

Stories to Read ABC 123

Fleming, Denise. *Count!* Holt, 1992. The antics of lively animals present the numbers 1–10, 20, 30, 50 and 100.

Rockwell, Anne. *Willy Can Count.* Arcade, 1989. Will bear and his mother observe many things to count, from buttons to bugs to birds.

Serfozo, Mary. *Who Wants One?* Macmillan, 1992. Rhymed text and illustrations introduce the numbers one to ten.

The Teddy Bear Counting Book. Dorling Kindersley, 1994. Color photographs of a variety of teddy bears show the numbers one to ten.

Tucker, Sian. *1 2 3 Count With Me.* Little Simon, 1996. From one soaring rocket to twenty presents, this brightly colored counting book has 39 lift the flaps to share.

VanFleet, Matthew. *One Yellow Lion.* Dial, 1996. A fold-out book explores numbers, colors, and animals.

One, Two, Buckle My Shoe

One, two, buckle my shoe.
Three, four, shut the door.
Five, six, pick up sticks.
Seven, eight, lay them straight.
Nine, ten, a big fat hen.
Eleven, twelve, books on shelves.
Thirteen, fourteen, stories in between.
[Song]

Number One, Touch Your Tongue

Number one, touch your tongue.
Number two, touch your shoe.
Number three, touch your knee.
Number four, touch the floor.
Number five, learn to jive.
Number six, learn to skip.
Number seven, looks towards heaven.
Number eight, are you late?
Number nine, touch your spine.
Number ten, that's the end!
(do actions as described)
[Action Rhyme]

Clap

(tune of "Row, Row, Row Your Boat")

Clap, clap, clap your hands,
Clap them one, two, three.
The more you clap,
The more you count,
So what will your count be?
[Song]

☺ **Story Souvenir:** Number coloring sheet
Photocopy the number sheet on the next page for children to color.

1234
567
890

Let's Eat

Stories to Read ABC 123

Fleming, Denise. *Lunch*. Holt, 1992. A very hungry mouse eats a large, colorful lunch.

Howard, Jean. *When I'm Hungry*. Dutton, 1992. A child imagines eating in the manner of a variety of animals.

Kasza, Keiko. *The Wolf's Chicken Stew*. Putnam, 1987. This wolf loves to eat, and tries to make chicken stew with surprising results.

Kennedy, Jimmy. *The Teddy Bear's Picnic*. Peter Bedrick, 1987. This book presents the text of the song about the secret teddy bear celebration.

Morris, Anne. *Bread, Bread, Bread*. Mulberry, 1989. This book celebrates many kinds of bread and how it is enjoyed the world over.

Rice, Eve. *Benny Bakes a Cake*. Greenwillow, 1981. When the dog eats Benny's birthday cake, dad comes to the rescue.

Watanabe, Shigeo. *What a Good Lunch*. Philomel, 1979. A baby bear demonstrates the right and wrong way to dress.

Wheeler, Cindy. *Marmalade's Picnic*. Knopf, 1982. Marmalade the orange cat has a picnic.

Popcorn

Pop, pop, pop! *(clap hands)*
Pour the corn into the pot.
Pop, pop, pop! *(clap hands)*
Take and shake it until it's hot.
Pop, pop, pop! *(clap hands)*
Lift the lid—what have you got?
Pop, pop, pop! *(clap)* Popcorn!
[Action Rhyme]

Picnic

(tune of "Here We Go Round the Mulberry Bush")

Here we go on a picnic today,
Picnic today, picnic today.
Here we go on a picnic today
So early in the morning.
Repeat with "This is the way we eat our food."
[Song]

Five Little Cookies

Five little cookies with frosting galore,
Mother ate one and then there were four.
Four little cookies, two and two you see,
Father ate one and then there were three.
Three little cookies, but before I knew,
Sister ate one and then there were two.
Two little cookies, yum, yum, yum,
Brother ate one and then there was one.
One little cookie, here I come,
I ate it, now there are none.
(Hold up five, four, three, two, and one fingers.)
[Fingerplay]

☺ **Story Souvenir:** <u>Place Mats</u>
Photocopy the place mat pattern on the next page for children to color.

My Place Mat

Library Time

Freeman, Don. *Quiet! There's a Canary in the Library*. Golden Gate, 1969. A girl dreams about the animal day she would have at the library if she were the librarian.

Huff, Barbara. *Once Inside the Library*. Little Brown, 1985. A descriptive poem tells of the joys of books, the library, and reading.

Numeroff, Laura. *Beatrice Doesn't Want To.* Franklin Watts, 1981. Beatrice doesn't like books or the library until she is forced to visit one Saturday and discovers the children's room.

Porte, Barbara. *Harry in Trouble*. Greenwillow, 1989. Harry is upset about losing his library card three times in a row until he finds out that others lose things too.

Radlauer, Ruth. *Molly at the Library*. Simon & Schuster, 1988. Four-year-old Molly visits the library with her father and is thrilled to find out that she can borrow ten books for fourteen days.

Five Little Books

Five little books,
Sitting on a shelf.
Look inside,
And see a little elf.
Four little books,
All in a row.
Look inside,
See it start to snow.
Three little books,
Still on the shelf.
Can you take one,
And read it for yourself?
Two little books,
Left on the pile.
Find one now,
And read it with a smile.
One little book,
All that is there.
Found itself a reader,
Who was happy to share.
[Fingerplay]

Over the Street and Through the Town

(To the tune of "Over the River and Through the Woods.")

Over the street and through the town
To the library we go,
Dad knows the way
To travel each day
Because we love to go-oh!
Over the street and through the town
To the library we go;
There are so many books
That I'm going to look
And so much I will know!
[Song]

Here Is My Book

Here is my book
(hold hands as if holding closed book)
I open it wide, *(pretend to open book)*
To see the pictures,
That are inside.
[Fingerplay]

☀ **Story Souvenir:**
Librarian coloring sheet

Mice

Boyd, Lizi. *Mouse in the House.* Little Brown, 1993. A wonderful book that comes with a stuffed gray mouse. This book unfolds to show mouse's house and to tell a story about what mouse does at home.

Butler, Stephen. *The Mouse and the Apple.* Tambourine, 1994. Other animals come and go, but mouse waits patiently for the ripe apple to fall from the tree.

Dunbar, Joyce. *Ten Little Mice.* Harcourt Brace Jovanovich, 1990. This book follows the activities of ten little mice as one by one they scurry home.

Kraus, Robert. *Whose Mouse Are You?* Macmillan, 1970. A lonely mouse resourcefully brings his family back together.

Polushkin, Maria. *Mother, Mother, I Want Another.* Crown, 1978. Mrs. Mouse tries to get baby mouse to go to sleep, but he "wants another mother!"

Walsh, Ellen. *Mouse Count.* Harcourt Brace Jovanovich, 1991. Ten little mice outsmart a very hungry snake.

Wood, Don. *The Little Mouse, the Big Bear, and the Ripe Red Strawberry.* Child's Play, 1984. A mouse picks a ripe, red delicious strawberry and tries to hide it from a hungry bear.

Tiny Mouse

There is such a tiny mouse,
(make little mouse with fingers)
Living quietly in my house.
Out at night he starts to creep, *(creep fingers)*
When everyone is fast asleep. *(pretend to sleep)*
But always by the light of day,
(circle arms over head to form sun)
The mouse quietly, quietly creeps away.
(creep fingers again)
[Fingerplay]

Hickory Dickory Dock

Hickory dickory dock,
(bend at waist and swing arms)
The mouse ran up the clock, *("run" fingers up arm)*
The clock struck one, *(clap on one)*
The mouse ran down,
Hickory, dickory, dock!
[Action Rhyme]

☼ **Story Souvenir:**
Baby mouse coloring sheet

Monkeyshines

Stories
to Read ABC
123

Christelow, Eileen. *Five Little Monkeys Jumping on the Bed*. Clarion, 1989. A counting book in which each of five monkeys falls off the bed and bumps his head. (I)

Kepes, Juliet. *Run, Little Monkeys, Run, Run, Run!* Pantheon, 1974. Three monkeys escape from three very hungry leopards.

Magni, Laura. *Two Little Monkeys.* Boyd Mills, 1996. A fold-out book featuring two monkeys on their way to the beach.

Oeschsli, Kelly. *Too Many Monkeys.* Golden Press, 1980. Monkeys frolic up to ten and down again.

Perkins, Al. *Hand, Hand, Fingers, Thumb.* Random House, 1969. Easy-to-read rhymed text has a monkey describing what can be done on a drum with a hand, fingers, and thumb.

Sachar, Louis. *Monkey Soup.* Knopf, 1992. With the help of a toy monkey, a girl makes a soup full of band-aids, crayons, and tissues for her father who is sick in bed. *Note: Makes a good flannel board story.*

Slobodkina, Esyphr. *Caps for Sale.* Harper & Row, 1947. A band of mischievous monkeys steal every one of a peddler's caps while he sleeps under a tree.

Five Little Monkeys in a Tall Tree

Five little monkeys in a tall tree,
(hold up five fingers)
Old Mr. Crocodile can't catch me.
(shake head no)
Along comes Mr. Crocodile and *SNAP!*
(open and close arms as if a crocodile mouth)
Four little monkeys.
(hold up four fingers)

Repeat with four, three, two, one.
[Action Rhyme]

I'm a Little Monkey

I'm a little monkey,
(point to self)
Watch me play.
(hop around)
Munching on bananas,
Every day.
(pretend to eat bananas)
I have a monkey friend,
Who plays with me.
(hop again)
Watch us as we,
Climb a tree.
(pretend to climb tree)
[Action Rhyme]

Monkey Man

(To the tune of "Muffin Man.")
Come and play,
Awhile with me,
Underneath the
Monkey tree.
Monkey see,
Monkey do,
Just like monkeys
In the zoo.
[Song]

☻ **Story Souvenir:** <u>Monkey sack puppet</u>
Photocopy the monkey face on the following page and cut out. Glue it to the flat bottom of a lunch sack. Glue a piece of yarn on the back of the sack as a tail.

Moonlight & Midnight

Aaragon, Jane. *Salt Hands.* Dutton, 1989. The gentle tale of a young girl who befriends a stag.

Arnosky, Jim. *All Night Near the Water.* Putnam, 1994. A family of baby ducks stays awake under the care of their mother all night long.

———. *Raccoons and Ripe Corn.* Lothrop, 1987. Hungry raccoons feast at night in a cornfield.

Pandell, Karen. *I Love You Sun, I Love You Moon.* Putnam, 1994. Expressions of love for nature in boardbook format.

Sampton, Sheila. *Moon to Sun.* Boyd Mills, 1993. From the stillness of the moon light to the break of day, each page adds an object to the landscape.

Wahl, Jan. *Cabbage Moon.* Holt, 1965. Princess Adelgitha and her dog Jenny love the moon, which looks like a cabbage, until it is stolen from the sky for a salad.

Weiss, Nicki. *Where Does the Brown Bear Go?* Greenwillow, 1989. When night comes, all of the animals find their way home. (I)

Moon

Moon, moon,
(form moon overhead with arms)
Up so high, *(point up)*
Big white moon,
(form moon again)
In a big, black sky.

Moon, moon, *(form moon overhead)*
Beautiful one, *(hold up one finger)*
Following the setting sun.
(form moon again and lean to the side)
[Rhyme]

Deer Dream

One night I dreamed of a little deer,
That had tiny horns on it's head.
(hold hands on head to make antlers)
I rode on it's back as I dreamed along,
(pretend to ride)
But when I woke up, it was gone.
[Action Rhyme]

☼ **Story Souvenir:** Deer finger puppet
Photocopy the deer pattern onto brown paper and cut out. Attach to the children's fingers with tape.

Little Deer

Out in the forest
Early in the day
(form sun over head with arms)
See the deer
(hold up one hand with two fingers up for antlers)
As it plays.
She eats some leaves
And then some grass
(pretend to eat)
I wave to her
As she runs past.
(wave)
[Fingerplay]

Mother Goose

Cousins, Lucy. *Jack and Jill and Other Nursery Rhymes.* Dutton, 1996. Board book of brightly illustrated rhymes.

Dr. Hickey. *Mother Goose and More.* Additions, 1990. Nursery rhymes with additional lines added.

Galdone, Paul. *Little Bo Peep.* Clarion, 1986. An illustrated rendition of the rhyme about the little girl who loses her sheep. (I)

Gill, Sheila. *The Alaska Mother Goose.* Paws IV, 1987. Nursery rhymes featuring Alaskan animals.

Henessey, B. G. *The Missing Tarts.* Viking Kestrel, 1989. The Queen of Hearts asks a variety of fairy tale characters to help her find her missing tarts.

Kessler, Leonard. *Hey Diddle Diddle.* Garrard, 1980. The traditional Mother Goose rhyme is expanded with some very silly verses.

McKellar, Shona. *Counting Rhymes.* Dorling Kindersley, 1990. Counting rhymes such as "I Saw Three Ships" and "This Old Man" illustrated with color photographs.

Nightingale, Sandy. *A Giraffe on the Moon.* Harcourt Brace Jovanovich, 1991. The images of a young child's dream include a giraffe on the moon, a cat in a balloon, and other rhyming things. (I)

Rosenberg, Liz. *Mama Goose.* Philomel, 1994. A collection of well- and lesser-known nursery rhymes.

Five Fat Peas

Five fat peas in a pea pod pressed,
(Hold one hand over the other to form a pod)
One grew, two grew,
(Extend thumbs and index fingers together)
And so did all the rest.
(Raise middle, ring, and little fingers in turn)
They grew, and they grew,
(Pull hands apart slowly)
And they grew, and they grew,
And they grew so fat and portly,
That the pea pod POPPED!
(Finish with a loud pop)
[Rhyme]

I'm a Little Teapot

I'm a little teapot, short and stout.
Here is my handle, here is my spout.
When I get all steamed up hear me shout,
"Just tip me over and pour me out."
[Song]

Hey Diddle Diddle

(Use the patterns to create stick puppets for the children to hold as you recite the rhyme. Use a real spoon for the spoon and a paper plate for the dish.)

Hey diddle diddle,
The cat played the fiddle,
The cow jumped over the moon.
The little dog laughed,
To see such sport,
And the dish ran away with the spoon!
[Rhyme]

 Story Souvenir: Mother Goose coloring sheet

Multicultural

Agell, Charlotte. *Dancing Feet.* Gulliver, 1994. Rhymed text celebrates the diversity of the world's cultures.

Baer, Edith. *This Is the Way We Eat Our Lunch.* Scholastic, 1995. Relates in rhyme what children eat in countries around the world.

Chocolate, Debbie. *Kente Colors.* Walker, 1996. A rhyming description of Kente cloth costumes of Ghana, including the meaning of the colors and patterns.

Hamanaka, Sheila. *All the Colors of the Earth.* Morrow, 1994. This book reveals in rhyme that despite all their outer differences, kids all over the world are lovable.

Leventhal, Debra. *What is Your Language?* Dutton, 1994. This book emphasizes the many languages spoken around the world.

Martin, Bill. *Here Are My Hands.* Lothrop, 1987. The owner of this human body celebrates it's parts and what they do.

Morris, Anne. *Loving.* Lothrop, Lee, and Shepherd, 1987. Color photographs provide examples of the many different ways love is expressed.

Five Lovely Children

Five lovely children stand in a row.
(Hold up five fingers)
The first one's hair is tied in a bow.
(Raise respective fingers)
The second one's hands are in his lap.
The third one wears a colorful cap.
The fourth one says "Have a nice day."
The fifth one says "Now we all can play!"
[Fingerplay]

Music: Sing "Go in and Out the Village" from the cassette **Wee Sing and Play** by Pamela Beall. Price Stern Sloan, 1989. Encourage participation by children with the help of their adults.

Children of the World

Trace the following children patterns onto flannel or Pellon (sew-in fabric interfacing). Color with markers or colored pencils. Use the rhyme that follows as you display the children on a flannelboard or storytelling apron.

This boy lives in the USA
This girl is from Mexico.
This boy lives in Norway
And she calls China home.
All of the children of the world, you see,
Are part of the Earth's great family.
[Flannelboard Rhyme]

☼ **Story Souvenir:** Hands and hearts
Place a child's hand on a folded piece of red construction paper as shown in the illustration. The index finger should be bent to touch the fold as should the tip of the thumb. Trace around the child's hand with a pencil. Cut the pattern out around the outside and between the index finger and thumb. When the paper is unfolded the empty space between the finger and thumb will form a heart.

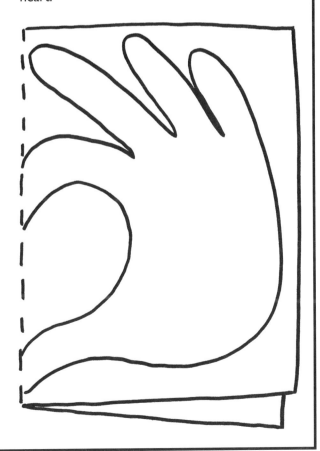

My Blanket

Brady, Susan. *Find My Blanket.* Lippincott, 1990. Sam Mouse hates to miss fun by going to bed, so he hides his own blanket and asks his family to look for it.

Graham, Bob. *The Red Woolen Blanket.* Little Brown, 1988. Julia carries her blanket everywhere until one day she outgrows it.

Jonas, Anne. *Where Can It Be?* Greenwillow, 1986. A child's search for a missing blanket is depicted with simple illustrations.

Keller, Holly. *Geraldine's Blanket.* Greenwillow, 1984. When her her parents insist that she must get rid of her baby blanket, Geraldine finds a clever way to keep it.

Stepto, Michelle. *Snuggle Piggy and the Magic Blanket.* Dutton, 1987. Snuggle Piggy must rescue his very special quilt from the rain. *Note: Makes a good flannel board story.*

Worth, Bonnie. *Bye, Bye Blankie.* Muppet/ Golden Press, 1992. Baby Muppet Piggy outgrows her blanket.

Blanket Colors

I once had a blanket,
It was fluffy and new.
I once had a blanket,
And it's color was _____. *(blue)*

I once had a blanket,
The prettiest I've seen.
I once had a blanket,
And it's color was _____. *(green)*

I once had a blanket,
Soft as a pillow.
I once had a blanket,
And it's color was _____. *(yellow)*

I once had a blanket,
At the foot of my bed.
I once had a blanket,
And it's color was _____. *(red)*

Use the pattern to create a flannel board for this rhyme. Make four blankets and color one red, yellow, green and blue. Place on the flannel board as you recite and encourage children to say the color names.
[Rhyme]

Music: "Blanket for a Sail" from *For Our Children,* Walt Disney, Inc., 1991.

☼ **Story Souvenir:**
<u>Snuggle Piggy coloring sheet</u>
Photocopy the Snuggle Piggy on the next page for children to color.

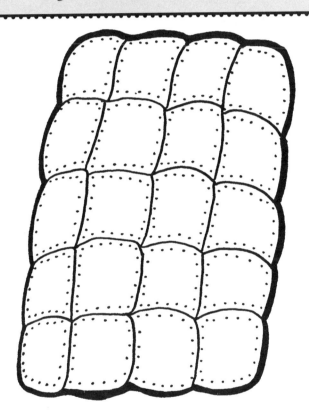

My Blanket

I have a little blanket,
Just for me.
Brother's too big for it,
Mommy's too big for it,
Daddy's too big for it,
Don't you see?
I have a little blanket,
Don't you see?
But kitty's too small for it,
Puppy's too small for it,
Baby's too small for it—
It's just for me!
[Rhyme]

Michele Stepto

74   My Blanket: Snuggle Piggy coloring sheet

On the Farm

STories to Read ABC 123

Baker, Keith. *Big Fat Hen*. Harcourt Brace Jovanovich, 1994. The traditional rhyme "One Two, Buckle My Shoe" is presented here featuring illustrations of charming baby chicks.

Brown, Margaret. *Big Red Barn*. HarperCollins, 1989. Rhymed text and illustrations introduce the many animals that live in the big red barn

Fleming, Denise. *Barnyard Banter*. Holt, 1994. All the barnyard animals are where they should be, each making their own distinct sound, except for the goose.

Lille, Patricia. *When the Rooster Crows.* Greenwillow, 1991. A farmer is unable to wake up in the morning until all his animals have joined voices with the rooster.

Luton, Mildred. *Little Chicks Mothers and All the Others.* Viking, 1983. Verses describe the animals that live on the farm and their young.

Miller, Jane. *Farm Noises.* Simon & Schuster, 1988. Color photographs depict animals and machines on a farm along with the distinct sounds they make.

Powell, Richard. *Baa! Who's On the Farm?* Little Simon, 1994. A guessing lift-the-flap book featuring a fuzzy sheep on the front.

Tucker, Sian. *Busy Farm: A Pop-Up Book.* Simon & Schuster, 1995. There is much to do on this busy movable farm—slide the ducks, turn the tractor wheels, and lift the flaps to see the farm animals.

Barnyard Song

(To the tune of "If You're Happy and You Know It")

If you're a chicken and you know it say, "cluck cluck."
If you're a chicken and you know it say, "cluck cluck."
If you're a chicken and you know it, then you really ought to show it.
If you're a chicken and you know it say, "cluck cluck."

Repeat with "pig, say oink oink,"" "cow, say moo moo, etc."
[Song]

This Little Cow

This little cow eats grass.
This little cow eats hay.
This little cow drinks water.
This little cow runs away.
And this little cow does nothing,
But lie and sleep all day,
MOO!
(hold up five fingers and bend down one for each cow)
[Fingerplay]

Farmer

Here is the farmer.
What does he do?
He feeds the cows,
And milks them, too.
Chickens and pigs,
Horses and sheep,
He puts in the barn,
So they can sleep.
[Rhyme]

☼ **Story Souvenir:** <u>Cow puppet</u>
Photocopy the cow pattern onto white paper. Let each child draw spots on their cow. Tape to craft sticks.

On the Go

Stories to Read ABC 123

Barton, Byron. *Trains.* Crowell, 1986. Brief text and brightly colored illustrations present a variety of trains and tell what they do.

Crews, Donald. *Freight Train.* Greenwillow, 1978. A colorful pictorial work with simple words about a train.

Dodds, Dayle Ann. *Wheel Away!* Harper & Row, 1989. A runaway wheel takes a bouncy, bumpy, noisy ride.

Levinson, Ricki. *I Go With My Family to Grandma's.* Dutton, 1986. Five cousins and their families arrive at Grandma's house using various means of transportation.

Shaw, Nancy. *Sheep in a Jeep.* Houghton Mifflin, 1986. The story of the misadventures of a group of sheep who are not very skilled at driving.

Williams, Sue. *I Went Walking.* Harcourt Brace Jovanovich, 1986. During the course of a walk, a young boy identifies animals of different colors.

A Walking We Will Go
(To the tune of "A Hunting We Will Go.")

A walking we will go,
A walking we will go,
We will walk and then we run,
A walking we will go!
[Song]

Here Is the Engine

Here is the engine on the track. *(thumb)*
Here is the coal car, just in back. *(pointer)*
Here is the boxcar to carry the freight. *(middle finger)*
Here is the mail car, don't be late! *(ring finger)*
Way back here at the end of the train
Rides the caboose through the sun and rain. *(pinky)*
[Fingerplay]

Traveling

I walk on legs, I ride a bicycle.
(pretend to walk then ride)
I drive a car, it's a fine vehicle.
(pretend to drive)
Go for a ride on a great big bus,
Wave at people, they wave at us. *(wave)*
These are a few ways to get to a place,
Including a rocket to outer space!
(form a rocket cone over head with arms)
[Action Rhyme]

☺ **Story Souvenir:** <u>Train coloring sheet</u>

Ouchies & Boo-Boos

Brandenburg, Franz. *I Wish I Was Sick, Too.* Morrow, 1990. A young child sees the special treatment a sibling gets when ill and wishes to be sick also.

Christelow, Eileen. *Five Little Monkeys Jumping on the Bed.* Clarion, 1989. A counting book in which each of five monkeys falls off the bed and bump heads. (I)

Loomis, Christine. *One Cow Coughed.* Ticknor and Fields, 1994. Animals count from one to ten and then back down again as they show symptoms of illness, then take care of themselves and get well.

Oxenbury, Helen. *The Checkup.* Puffin, 1994. A board book shows baby's first doctor visit. (I)

Rockwell, Anne. *Sick in Bed.* Macmillan, 1982. A little boy describes his experiences while being sick with a sore throat.

Roddie, Shen. *Chicken Pox.* Little Brown, 1993. Baby Chick tries to get rid of his itchy spots in this lift-the-flap and pull-the-tab book.

Tarsky, Sue. *Kiss the Boo-Boo.* Viking, 1997. An interactive book featuring a reusable bandage sticker. This book will inspire the reader to sooth the baby's cut.

Wescott, Nadine. *The Lady with the Alligator Purse.* Little Brown, 1988. The rhyme about the baby with humorous illustrations.

Five Little Monkeys

Five little monkeys,
(hold up five fingers)
Jumping on the bed,
(bounce hand)
One fell off,
And hurt his head.
(put hands on head)
Too him to the doctor,
(rock arms as if holding baby)
And the doctor said,
"No more monkeys
Jumping on the bed!"

Repeat with four, three, two, one, none.
[Fingerplay]

Terrible Cold

I have a terrible cold in my head,
(tap nose)
Ah-choo! Ah-choo!
So now I have to stay in bed.
Ah-choo! Ah-choo!
I went outside without my coat,
Sniffle, sniffle,
And now I have a very sore throat.
(rub throat)
[Action Rhyme]

If You Please

If you cough,
Or if you sneeze,
Cover your mouth,
Would you please?
[Rhyme]

Sore Toe

This little dog had a sore toe.
This little dog said, *"Oh, no!"*
This little dog said, *"That's bad."*
This little dog cried, *"How sad!"*
This little dog, helpful and good,
Ran for the nurse as fast as he could.
(hold up fingers 1–5)
[Fingerplay]

Jack and Jill

Jack and Jill,
Went up the hill, *(skip in place)*
To fetch a pail of water.
Jack fell down,
And broke his crown, *(put hands on head)*
And Jill came tumbling after. *(fall to ground)*
[Action Rhyme]

☼ **Story Souvenir:** <u>Band-aid</u>
Use the pattern to create band aids or give out real band aids that have decorations on them.

Owls

Stories to Read ABC 123

Hendra, Sue. *Oliver's Wood.* Candlewick, 1996. Oliver Owl stays up so late he sees the sun rise, but all his nocturnal friends are too busy sleeping to discuss it with him.

Hutchins, Pat. *Goodnight Owl.* Macmillan, 1972. All of the animals noise keep Owl awake during the day, but at night he gets his revenge.

Kraus, Robert. *Owliver.* Windmill, 1974. Owlivers parents try to tell him what to be when he grows up, but in the end he makes the decision.

Lear, Edward. *The Owl and the Pussycat.* Lothrop, 1991. After a courtship of a year and a day, Owl and Pussy get a ring from Pig and then marry.

McDonald, Megan. *Who-oo Is It?* Orchard, 1992. Mother Owl hears a mysterious noise and tries to identify it.

Thaler, Mike. *Owly.* Harper & Row, 1982. When Owly asks his mother question after question about the world, she finds just the right way to help him find answers.

Five Little Owls

(Use the owl pattern to create flannel board owl for this fingerplay)

This little owl was sitting on a limb.
This one flew over to play with him.
This owl was calling, "Whoo, whoo, whoo."
This one answered "I wish I knew."
"The sun's coming up," this one said,
And five little owls went to bed.
(hold up five fingers one at a time)
[Fingerplay]

Owlie

(To the tune of "Pop Goes the Weasel.")

An owl sat on the branch of a tree,
And was as quiet as can be.
The moon came out,
The night was dark—
"Whoo!" said the Owlie.
[Song]

Little Owl

There was a little owl,
Who lived in a tree.
She could see things,
That others could not see.
Hello, little owl,
Won't you answer me?
What do you see
From the top of your tree?
[Rhyme]

☀ **Story Souvenir:** <u>Owl puppet</u>
Photocopy the owl pattern onto brown or grey paper and cut it out. Tape to craft sticks.

Pandas

Calmenson, Stephanie. *Dinner at the Panda Palace.* HarperCollins, 1991. Mr. Panda manages to find seats for all his restaurant guests on a busy night.

Gackenback, Dick. *Poppy the Panda.* Clarion, 1984. Poppy is such a picky dresser that Katie can't satisfy his taste in clothing until mother comes up with a solution.

Hoban, Tana. *Panda, Panda.* Greenwillow, 1986. Black and white photographs show pandas in a zoo habitat.

Krauss, Robert. *Milton the Early Riser.* Windmill, 1972. Milton the panda wakes up very early and has no one to play with.

Leedy, Loreen. *Pingo, the Plaid Panda.* Henry Holt, 1988. Pingo is convinced that the other panda children will not play with him because he is plaid.

Owen, Annie. *Hungry Panda.* Kingfisher, 1997. An exuberant toy panda eats in a simple story. (I)

Stimson, Joan. *Big Panda, Little Panda.* Barron's, 1994. After the arrival of a new baby, Little Panda is now called Big Panda, and has some trouble adjusting to the change.

Five Little Panda Bears

Five little panda bears,
And no more.
One waddled off,
And then there were four.
Four little panda bears,
Sleeping in a tree.
One fell out,
And then there were three.
Three little panda bears,
Said "What can we do?"
One ate some bamboo leaves,
And then there were two.
Two little panda bears,
Playing in the sun.
One heard his mother growl,
And then there was one.
One little panda bear,
Left all alone.
He got up,
And ran right home.
[Fingerplay]

Panda Pokey

Sing the song "Hokey Pokey"
substituting the words "Panda Pokey."
Name panda body parts such as snout,
black ears, white tummy, black tail, etc.
[Action Song]

☼ **Story Souvenir:** Panda masks

Photocopy and enlarge the mask pattern. Punch a hole on each cheek and add yarn. Use a pencil to punch eye holes. Use the yarn ties to secure masks.

Panda in the Forest

A panda in the forest,
Roams among the green.
A panda in the forest,
Roams among the green.
A panda in the forest,
Roams among the green.
Looking for bamboo to eat.
She finds bamboo and eats it.
She finds bamboo and eats it.
She finds bamboo and eats it.
Yummy bamboo to eat.
[Rhyme]

Piggies

STories to Read **ABC** **123**

Degen, Bruce. *Sailaway Home*. Scholastic Inc., 1996. A young pig imagines adventures in the sea and sky, always returning home at days end.

Galdone, Paul. *The Three Little Pigs*. Houghton Mifflin, 1987. The traditional folk tale about the hungry wolf and tricky pigs.

Kasza, Keiko. *The Pig's Picnic*. Putnam, 1988. Mr. Pig, in an attempt to impress Miss Pig, borrows various parts from animals friends with alarming results.

McPhail, David. *Pigs Aplenty, Pigs Galore*. Macmillan, 1993. One night, a man hears the sound of eating and soon his house is filled with messy pigs.

Pomerantz, Charlotte. *Piggy in the Puddle*. Mcmillan, 1974. A lilting rhyme tells of a pig in a mud puddle who will not get out and take a bath. *Note: Makes a good flannel board story.*

Wood, Audrey. *Piggies!* Harcourt Brace Jovanovich, 1991. Ten little piggies dance and play on a child's toes before going to sleep.

This Little Piggy

This little piggy went to market.
This little piggy stayed home.
This little piggy had roast beef.
This little piggy had none.
And this little piggy went wee-wee-wee-wee
All the way home.
[Fingerplay]

Down in the Barnyard
(To the tune of "Down By the Station.")

Down in the barnyard,
Early in the morning,
See the little piggies,
All in a row.
Oink-oink, snort-snort,
Is how they go!
[Song]

Pig on the Farm

Down by the farm
We love to play
In the mud puddle
All the day.
Down in the mud
We like to roll
Until we are
As black as coal.
[Rhyme]

☼ **Story Souvenir:** Pig puppet
Photocopy the pig pattern onto pink paper and cut out. Tape to craft sticks.

Pumpkins

Hall, Lynn. *It's Pumpkin Time.* Scholastic Inc., 1994. A sister and a brother plant their own pumpkin patch so that they will have a jack-o-lantern for Halloween.

Hutchings, Amy. *Picking Apples and Pumpkins.* Scholastic Inc., 1994. Spend the day with Kristy as her family picks apples and pumpkins at the Battleview orchard in New Jersey.

Oldfield, Pamela. *The Halloween Pumpkin.* Children's Press, 1976. A Halloween pumpkin manages to scare everyone except a hungry pig.

Rockwell, Anne. *Apples and Pumpkins.* Macmillan, 1989. A family visits Mr. Comstock's farm to pick apples and pumpkins.

Titherington, Jeannie. *Pumpkin, Pumpkin.* Greenwillow, 1986. Jaime plants a pumpkin seed, waters it, watches it grow, harvests it, carves it for Halloween, and then saves some seeds for spring. (I)

I'm a Little Pumpkin

(To the tune of "I'm a Little Teapot.")

I'm a little pumpkin, fat and round.
Here is my face making a frown.
I'm a little pumpkin, tall and thin.
Here is my face making a grin.
I'm a little pumpkin, I've got style,
Here is my face making a smile!
[Song]

This Little Pumpkin

This little pumpkin was small and round.
This little pumpkin sat on the ground.
This little pumpkin was short and fat.
This little pumpkin wore a funny hat.
This little pumpkin had a smile so keen.
And they all said, "Happy Halloween."
(hold up one through five fingers in succession)
[Fingerplay]

Story Souvenir: Pumpkin finger puppet
Photocopy the pumpkin pattern onto orange paper and cut out. Attach to the children's fingers with tape.

Pumpkin, Pumpkin

Pumpkin, pumpkin,
Sitting on the wall.
(make a fist with one hand and put it on top of the other arm)
Pumpkin, pumpkin,
Tip and fall.
(make your fist fall off the arm)
Pumpkin, pumpkin,
Rolling down the street.
(roll one fist over the other)
Pumpkin, pumpkin,
Trick or treat!
[Action Rhyme]

Rabbits

Bornstein, Ruth. *Rabbit's Good News.* Clarion, 1995. Rabbit leaves her warm, dark burrow and discovers that spring has come.

Brown, Margaret. *Runaway Bunny.* Harper & Row, 1942. The classic tale of a bunny who asks questions about running away that his mother has all the answers for.

Capucilli, Alyssa. *Peekaboo Bunny: Friends in the Snow.* Scholastic Inc., 1995. It's winter and the ground is covered with snow. Lift the flaps and find Peekaboo Bunny and her animal friends.

Dodds, Dayle Ann. *Do Bunnies Talk?* HarperCollins, 1992. This book introduces a variety of human and animal sounds that bunnies do not make.

Gag, Wanda. *ABC Bunny.* Howard McCann, 1933. An alphabet featuring a rabbit.

LeTord, Bijou. *Rabbit Seeds.* Dell, 1984. A rabbit gardeners work lasts all year, from spring until fall.

Wellington, Monica. *Night Rabbits.* Penguin, 1985. Simple text and bright illustrations depict the typical night activities of young rabbits.

The Rabbit and the Snowman

A chubby little snowman,
(arms make a fat tummy)
Has a carrot nose, *(hold fist in front of nose)*
Along came a bunny,
(hold up two fingers and "hop" them)
And what do you suppose?
That hungry little bunny, *(rub tummy)*
Looking for his lunch,
(shade eyes and look around)
Ate the snowman's carrot nose
(hold fist in front of nose)
Nibble, nibble, *CRUNCH!* *(open and close hand, then put behind back)*
[Action Rhyme]

This Little Bunny

This little bunny has two pink eyes,
This little bunny is very wise.
This little bunny is soft as silk,
This little bunny is as white as milk.
This little bunny just nibbles away
At lettuce and carrots all the day.
(Hold up five fingers and bend each one down with each verse.)
[Fingerplay]

☼ **Story Souvenir:** Paper tube rabbit
Photocopy the rabbit head pattern onto white paper and cut out. Glue it to one end of a toilet paper tube. On the opposite side and end, glue a cotton ball to make a tail.

Hop!

(Make up a tune.)

Hop, hop, hop, hop, hop
Like a rabbit.
Hop, hop, hop, hop, hop
Like a rabbit.
Hop, hop, hop, hop, hop
Like a rabbit.
All around the room!
[Song]

Sheep

Stories
to Read
ABC 123

Alda, Arlene. *Sheep, Sheep, Sheep, Help Me Fall Asleep.* Delacorte, 1992. A child tries to count sheep to fall asleep, but sees many other animals first.

Archambault, John. *Counting Sheep.* Holt, 1989. Tired of counting sheep, a child counts other imaginative animals to help herself fall asleep.

Bursik, Rose. *Zoe's Sheep.* Holt, 1994. Zoe tries counting sheep to help her fall asleep, but these are rowdy noisy sheep

Hale, Sarah. *Mary Had a Little Lamb.* Scholastic, 1990. A contemporary interpretation of the nursery rhyme featuring color photographs by Bruce McMillan.

Shaw, Nancy. *Sheep on a Ship.* Houghton Mifflin, 1989. The same sheep from Sheep in a Jeep go on a sea voyage and run into a storm.

I Love Sheep

I love sheep.
I count them in my sleep.
(pretend to count)
They jump in the sky.
They jump very high.
(jump)
They help me to sleep.
(pretend to sleep)
So I love sheep.
[Fingerplay]

White Sheep

There was once a white sheep,
And this is the way
The shepherd cut off
His wool one day.
The wool was spun
Into yarn so fine
And knit into
This sweater of mine.
[Rhyme]

Baa Baa Black Sheep

Baa, baa black sheep,
Have you any wool?
Yes, sir, yes sir,
Three bags full.
One for my master,
One for my dame,
And one for the little boy
That lives down the lane.
[Song]

☼ **Story Souvenir:** <u>Sheep finger puppet</u>
Photocopy the sheep pattern onto white paper and cut out. Attach the finger puppet to the children's fingers using tape.

Snakes & Lizards

Baker, Keith. *Hide and Snake*. Harcourt Brace Jovanovich, 1991. A brightly colored snake challenges readers to a game of hide and seek as he hides among familiar objects.

Buchanan, Ken. *Lizards on the Wall*. Harbinger House, 1992. A humorous rhyme in which the observer tells the tale of the nightly battle between the lizards and the insects that live on a wall.

Carle, Eric. *The Mixed Up Chameleon*. Crowell, 1984. A chameleon wishes to be all of the animals he sees with mixed up results. Cut outs along the edge of the pages show each animal and it's color.

Gray, Linda. *Small Green Snake*. Orchard, 1994. Despite his mother's warnings, a small, green snake wanders away to explore the sounds he hears in the garden.

Leydenfrost, Robert. *The Snake That Sneezed*. Putnam, 1970. A snake goes out into the world to seek his fortune, but bites off more than he can chew.

Punnett, Dick. *Name Lizzy's Colors*. Children's Press, 1982. The reader helps Lizzy by telling her what color to change into to escape danger.

Walsh, Ellen. *Mouse Count. Mouse Count*. Harcourt Brace Jovanovich, 1991. Ten little mice outsmart a very hungry snake.

Snakes Slither

Snakes slither,
On the ground.
Snakes slither,
All around.
Some are short,
And all are thin.
They have sharp teeth,
To make a grin.
[Rhyme]

Sammy Snake

Sammy is a slippery snake.
(wiggle fingers on opposite palm)
He sleeps on the shore of a nice blue lake.
(curl fingers to show sleep)
He squirms and squiggles to catch a snack.
(wiggle fingers)
Then takes a nap till his hunger comes back.
(curl fingers)
[Fingerplay]

Snake

The sneaky, slithery, slippery snake,
(put palms together and move them side to side)
Slip through the grasses,
making them shake—SSSSSSSSSSSS!
[Action Rhyme]

Music: "I'm Being Eaten By a Boa Constrictor" from **Peter, Paul, and Mommy** by Peter, Paul, and Mary. Warner Brothers, 1969.

☺ **Story Souvenir:** <u>Green snake</u>
Photocopy the snake pattern onto green paper.
Cut out on the dotted lines.

Thanksgiving

Stories to Read ABC 123

Child, Lydia Marie. ***Over the River and Through the Wood.*** HarperCollins, 1992. The traditional Thanksgiving song is illustrated

Cuyler, Margery. ***Daisy's Crazy Thanksgiving.*** Henry Holt, 1990. Daisy tries to spend a quiet Thanksgiving away from her parent's restaurant, but finds her relatives are even more noisy.

Dragonwagon, Crescent. ***Alligator Arrived with Apples.*** Macmillan, 1992. From Alligator's apples to Zebra's zucchini, an alphabet of animals and food celebrate a Thanksgiving feast.

Hallinan, P.K. ***I'm Thankful Each Day.*** Hambleton Hill, 1989. A child tells of all the wonderful things in the world there are to be thankful for.

Niko-Lisa, W. ***1, 2, 3, Thanksgiving.*** Albert Whitman, 1991. This Thanksgiving counting book depicts the numbers one through ten through scenes of the holiday.

Ziefert, Harriet. ***What is Thanksgiving?*** HarperCollins, 1992. Lift the flaps as Little Mouse and her family prepare and eat Thanksgiving dinner.

Turkey

I met a turkey gobbler,
When I went out to play.
I asked him, "Mr. Turkey, how are you today?"
He said, "Don't ask me that question
On this Thanksgiving day!"
[Rhyme]

Turkey Trot

(To the tune of "Mulberry Bush.")

This is the way the turkey runs,
Turkey runs, turkey runs.
This is the way the turkey runs,
On Thanksgiving Day.

Repeat with "farmer chases,"
"turkey gobbles," etc.
[Song]

Ten Turkeys

Ten fat turkeys standing in a row,
(hold up ten fingers)
They spread their wings and their tails like so.
(spread fingers)
They strut to the left,
They strut to the right,
(move fingers left and right)
Then they say, "Gobble gobble gobble"
in the bright sunlight.
[Fingerplay]

☼ **Story Souvenir:** <u>Turkey coloring sheet</u>

Underwater

Stories to Read ABC 123

Arnosky, Jim. *Otters Underwater*. Putnam, 1992. This book shows two young otters frolicking and feeding in a pond.

Craig, Janet. *What's Under the Ocean?* Troll, 1982. Brief text and pictures show the plants and animals that live in the ocean.

Kalan, Robert. *Blue Sea*. Greenwillow, 1979. Progressively larger fish are chased by and escape from the biggest fish.

Martin, David. *The Fish Book*. Golden Press, 1964. A very basic introduction to animals that live in and around the sea. The book has very large pictures.

Ruschak, Lynette. *One Hot Day*. Artists and Writers Guild, 1994. One hot day, the shiniest jungle bug hops by the largest gorilla, setting off a pop up chain reaction.

Wylie, Joanne. *Fishy Color Story*. Children's Press, 1983. A child introduces the colors while answering questions about a beautiful fish.

Five Little Fishies

(Hold up five fingers. Start with thumb, and bend down fingers one at a time as rhyme progresses. Or, use the fish pattern to create a flannel board for this fingerplay.)

Five little fishes were swimming by the shore,
One took a dive and then there were four.
Four little fishes swimming out to sea,
One ate a worm and then there were three.
Three little fishes, said "Now what do we do?"
One swam away, and then there were two.
Two little fishes, having great fun,
One jumped into the air and then there was one.
One little fish, swimming in the sun,
He swam home and then there were none.
[Fingerplay]

Swimming

I hold my fingers like a fish
(place one hand on top of the other to form a fish shape)
And wave them as I go.
(move hands together in an up and down motion)
See them swim with a swish
Swiftly to and fro.
[Action Rhyme]

I'm a Little Fishy

(To the tune of "I'm a Little Teapot.")

I'm a little fishy, I can swim.
Here is my tail and here is my fin.
When I want to have fun with my friends,
I wiggle my tail and dive right in.
[Song]

☀ **Story Souvenir:** <u>Fish on a line</u>
Photocopy the fish pattern onto green or blue paper and cut it out. Tape on end of a 6' piece of yarn to the backside of the fish near the mouth. Tie the other end of the yarn to a craft stick to create a fish on a line.

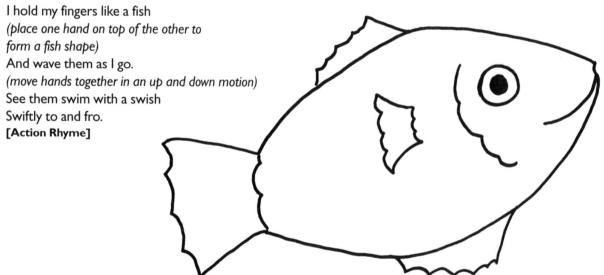

What Did Happen to the Dinosaurs?

Barton, Byron. *Dinosaurs.* HarperCollins, 1997. Vibrant illustrations and text appropriate for the very young identify dinosaurs in this board book.

——. *Dinosaurs, Dinosaurs.* HarperCollins, 1989. In prehistoric days, there were many kinds of dinosaurs-big or small, with sharp teeth or spikes.

Blumenthal, Nancy. *Count-a-saurus.* Four Winds, 1989. Numbered groups of dinosaurs and other prehistoric creatures count from one to ten.

Boynton, Sandra. *Oh My Oh My Oh Dinosaurs!* Workman, 1993. Dinosaurs do activities such as sunbathing and creating art in this board book.

Bram, Elizabeth. *A Dinosaur Is Too Big.* Greenwillow, 1977. A dinosaur makes a huge pet, but one that is lots of fun for a small child. *Note: This makes a good flannel board story.*

Carter, David. *What's in the Prehistoric Forest?* Holt, 1990. This lift the flap and pop up book shows several prehistoric creatures.

Otto, Carolyn. *Dinosaur Chase.* HarperCollins, 1991. A mother dinosaur tells her child a bedtime story about a stolen necklace and the resulting police chase.

Strickland, Paul. *Dinosaur Roar.* Dutton, 1994. Sweet, grumpy, spiky, and lumpy dinosaurs are all presented in rhyme.

Five Fat Funny Dinosaurs

Five fat funny dinosaurs, letting out a roar,
One went away and then there were four.
Four fat funny dinosaurs, munching on a tree,
One went away and then there were three.
Three fat funny dinosaurs, didn't know what to do,
One went away and then there were two.
Two fat funny dinosaurs, having lots of fun.
One went away and then there was one.
One fat funny dinosaur, walking in the sun.
He went home and then there were none!
[Fingerplay]

Dinosaurs

Dinosaurs were big,
Dinosaurs were loud!
Dinosaurs were scaly,
Dinosaurs were proud.
Even though we seen them no more,
Everyone loves a dinosaur!
[Rhyme]

Baby Dinosaur

(To the tune of "Baby Bumblebee.")

I'm bringing home a baby dinosaur,
Won't my mommy hide behind the door?
I'm bringing home a baby dinosaur,
Roar, roar, roar, roar!
[Song]

☼ **Story Souvenir:** Paper plate dinosaur
Trace or copy the pattern onto a 6" paper plate. Cut in half on the dotted line. Next, cut out the pieces on the solid lines. Tape or staple together and let the children color.

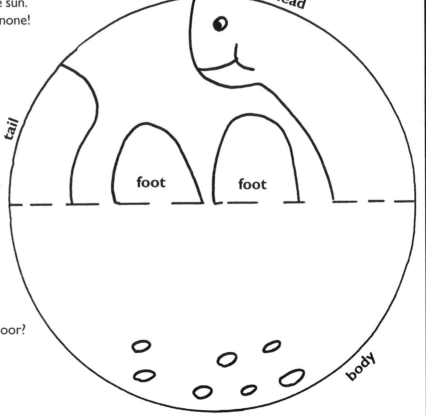

Zoo

Barton, Byron. *Zoo Animals*. HarperCollins, 1997. Vibrant illustrations and text appropriate for the very young identify zoo animals in this board book.

Campbell, Rod. *Dear Zoo*. Puffin, 1982. A child writes a letter to the zoo seeking the perfect pet. He gets many responses in this lift the flap book.

Carlstrom, Nancy. *What Would You Do If You Lived at the Zoo?* Little Brown, 1994. This book has die cut holes in the pages through which readers are invites to answer questions with animal sounds and actions.

Paterson, Bettina. *My First Animals*. Crowell, 1990. Paper cut illustrations depict well known animals in this bright book.

Powell, Richard. *Grrrr! Who's in the Jungle?* Little Simon, 1994. This book, which features a lion with touchable fur on the front, shows jungle animals under movable flaps.

Going to the Zoo
(To the tune of "Skip to My Lou.")

Come along children, we're going to the zoo.
Come along children, we're going to the zoo.
Come along children, we're going to the zoo.
Going to the zoo today!
[Song]

Giraffe

The giraffe is as tall as tall can be,
(stretch arms up)
He eats the leaves right off the trees.
(hold hand over head and open and close hand like a mouth)
His neck is long and his legs are, too.
(point to neck and legs)
And he can run faster than me or you.
(run in place)
[Action Rhyme]

Do Like the Animals

Hop, hop, hop, hop, hop like a bunny,
Run, run, run like a dog.
Walk, walk, walk, walk, walk like an elephant,
Jump, jump, jump like a frog.
Swim, swim, swim, swim, swim
 like a goldfish.
Fly, fly fly like a bird.
(do actions as indicated)
[Action Rhyme]

☼ **Story Souvenir:** <u>Zoo animal finger puppets</u>
Photocopy the patterns on colored paper and cut out. Attach to the children's fingers with tape.

Resource Bibliography

Music for Infants & Toddlers

Action Songs for Special Occasions. (cassette) Kimbo, 1970. Twenty-three original children's holiday songs with fingerplays and games.

Beall, Pamela. *Wee Sing Fun and Folk*. (cassette book) Price Stern Sloane, 1989. The book contains lyrics, music, and activity suggestions for seventeen short folk songs.

Brand, Oscar. *I Sing, You Sing, We All Sing*. (compact disk) PPI, 1987. CD and song booklet features very familiar sing along songs.

A Child's First Nursery Songs. (video) Golden Book Video, 1990. A bear family spends the day with such favorite songs as "The Old Woman Who Lived in a Shoe," "Pease Porridge Hot," and others.

Disney Children's Favorites, 1 and 2. (compact disks) Walt Disney, 1979. A collection of familiar children's short songs.

Hallum, Rosemary. *Fingerplay Fun*. (cassette) Educational Activity Records, 1979. Activity songs for fun and learning, such as "Ten Little Indians," "Mr. Left and Mr. Right," and "Eency Weency Spider."

McGrath, Bob. *Songs and Games for Toddlers*. (cassette) Kids Records, 1985. Songs by Katherine Smithrim for preschool classes sung by Bob of Sesame Street fame.

Parker, Phillip A. *Barney's Favorites*, Vol. 1. (cassette) Lyons Partnership, 1993. Songs featuring the voice of Barney, such as "Looby Loo," "Bingo," and the "Barney Theme Song."

Polansky, Davis. *Animal Alphabet Songs*. (cassette) Perfect Score, 1982. An alphabet of songs about animals, from alligator to zebra.

Sharon, Lois, and Bram. *Mainly Mother Goose*. (cassette) Elephant Records, 1984. Mother Goose sing along songs.

Smithrim, Katherine. *Songs and Games for Toddlers*.

(video) Golden Book Video, 1986. The video version of the cassette.

Stewart, Georgianna. *Pre-K Hooray!* (cassette) Kimbo, 1993. Songs that promote listening, movement, self esteem, etc.

Movement and Song Books

Aliki. *Go Tell Aunt Rhody*. Macmillan, 1974. Illustrated version of the folk song.

Brown, Marc. *Play Rhymes*. Dutton, 1987. A collection of twelve play rhymes to be sung with illustrations to demonstrate the accompanying physical movements.

Shannon, George. *Oh, I Love!* Bradbury, 1989. A lullaby repeats the sound made by a rooster, pig, chic, goose, lamb, and a little baby.

Songs from Mother Goose. Compiled by Nancy Larrick. Harper and Row, 1989. A collection of Mother Goose rhymes including music, illustrations, and historical notes.

Warren, Jean. *Piggyback Songs for Infants and Toddlers*. Warren House, 1985. A collection of simple songs about everyday activities and objects set to familiar tunes.

Weiss, Nicki. *If You're Happy and You Know It*. Greenwillow, 1987. An illustrated collection of camp and traditional songs with piano and guitar music, featuring "Pop! Goes the Weasel," and "Do Your Ears Hang Low."

Books to Use with Props

Bornstein, Ruth. *Little Gorilla*. Seabury, 1976. Everyone in the jungle loves little gorilla, even after he grows up.(stuffed jungle animals)

Dunbar, Joyce. *Ten Little Mice*. Harcourt Brace Jovanovich, 1990. This story follows the activities of ten mice as one by one they scurry home. (ten stuffed mice)

Ehlert, Lois. *Growing Vegetable Soup*. Harcourt

Brace Jovanovich, 1987. A father and child grow vegetables and then make soup. (garden tools, seeds, can of soup)

Galdone, Paul. *The Little Red Hen*. Seabury Press, 1973. The traditional tale of the hen with lazy roommates. (hen, dog, cat, and mouse finger puppets)

————. *The Three Little Pigs*. Houghton Mifflin, 1987. The traditional folk tale about the hungry wolf and tricky pigs. (three pigs and wolf masks)

Ginsburg, Mirra. *Good Morning, Chick*. Greenwillow, 1980. When a newly hatched chick tries to imitate the rooster, he falls into a puddle. (plastic egg and chick finger puppet)

Kalan, Robert. *Blue Sea*. Greenwillow, 1979. Progressively larger fish are chased by and escape from the biggest fish. (fish stick puppets)

Kuskin, Karla. *Roar and More*. Harper & Row, 1990. Rhymed text presents behavior and noises of various zoo animals. (stuffed zoo animals)

Leydenfrost, Robert. *The Snake That Sneezed*. Putnam, 1970. A snake goes out into the world to seek his fortune, but bites off more than he can chew. (a hollow stuffed snake and various stuffed animals that will fit inside of it)

Nodset, Joan. *Who Took the Farmer's Hat?* HarperCollins, 1962. A farmer looks all over for his hat, but finds only various round, brown objects. (a round, brown, hat and plastic egg)

Pearson, Susan. *When Baby Went to Bed*. Viking Kestrel, 1987. One by one, ten animals climb into baby's bed at bedtime. (stuffed animals and blanket)

Walsh, Ellen. *Mouse Count*. Harcourt Brace Jovanovich, 1991. Ten little mice outsmart a hungry snake (snake, rock, and plastic mice)

Watanabe, Shigeo. *How Do I Put It On?* Philomel, 1979. A baby bear demonstrates the right and wrong ways to get dressed. (stuffed bear with clothes)

Wood, Don. *The Little Mouse, the Red, Ripe Strawberry, and the Big Hungry Bear*. Child's Play, 1984. A mouse picks a delicious strawberry and tries to hide it from a big, hungry bear. (stuffed mouse, bear mask, strawberry, plastic glasses with moustache)

Picture Books that Make Good Flannel Boards

Benjamin Allan. *Hallowhat?* Simon & Schuster, 1992. A rhymed board book featuring spooky Halloween creatures.

Boynton, Sandra. *But Not the Hippopotamus*. Little Simon, 1982. A group of common animals have fun together—but not the hippopotamus!

Bram, Elizabeth. *A Dinosaur Is Too Big*. Greenwillow, 1977. A dinosaur makes a huge pet, but one that is lots of fun for a small child.

Freeman, Don. *Quiet! There's a Canary in the Library*. Golden Gate, 1969. A girl dreams about the animal day she would have at the library if she were the librarian.

London, Johnathan. *Froggy Gets Dressed*. Puffin, 1996. Froggy wants to play in the snow, but is called back to put on more and more clothes by his mommy.

Morehead, Ruth. *A Christmas Countdown*. Random House, 1992. A rhymed countdown from ten colored Christmas balls to one Christmas tree.

Oldfield, Pamela. *The Halloween Pumpkin*. Children's Press, 1976. A Halloween pumpkin manages to scare everyone except the hungry pig.

Petie, Haris. *The Seed the Squirrel Dropped*. Prentice Hall, 1976. A tiny seed grows into—a cherry pie!

Pomerantz, Charlotte. *Piggy in a Puddle*. Macmillan, 1974. A lilting rhyme tells of a pig in a mud puddle who will not get out to take a bath.

Robart, Rose. *The Cake That Mack Ate*. Atlantic Monthly, 1987. A cumulative tale about a dog and a birthday cake.

Professional Resources

1001 Rhymes and Fingerplays. Warren House Publishing, 1994. A collection of fingerplays and actions rhymes on such topics as self, school, community, seasons, animals, plants, food, weather, earth and sky, holidays, special days, and special people.

Baby Einstein. Julie Clark Video, 1996. (http://www.babyeinstein.com:80/), 27 minutes. This video is made especially for young children, featuring color, sound, movement, faces, and other things that toddlers will recognize and respond to.

Bawden, Juliet. *Fun With Fabric*. Reed International, 1993. This book provides instructions on how to make things with fabric, including finger and glove puppets.

Brennan, Jan. *Treasured Time With Your Toddler*. August House, 1991. This monthly guide has suggested books, fingerplays, rhymes, songs, and other creative activities suitable for a toddler time.

Briggs, Diane. *Flannel Board Fun: A Collection of Stories, Songs, and Poems*. Scarecrow, 1992. A collection of stories, songs and poems for the flannel board.

————. *Toddler Storytime Programming*. Scarecrow Press, 1993. Suggested toddler time books, activities, and flannel boards.

Defty, Jeff. *Creative Finger Plays and Action Rhymes: An Index and Guide to their Uses.* Oryx, 1992. An extensive index of finger plays and action rhymes. 95 sources are indexed. This book also has several chapters on using fingerplays and rhymes as well as a collection of the better known fingerplays.

Jeffrey, Debby Ann. *Literate Beginnings: Programs for Babies and Toddlers.* ALA, 1995. Outlines for various toddler programs.

Morag, McLean, and others. "Rhymes, Nursery Rhymes, and Reading in Early Childhood." *Merrill Palmer Quarterly* 33(July 1987):255-81. This article explains the importance of rhymes to a child's early language development.

Nichols, Judy. *Storytimes for Two-Year-Olds.* ALA, 1987. One of the first and best books containing outlines for toddler story programs.

Noel, Karen. *Cut and Color Flannel Board Stories: Book 1 and 2.* T.S. Denison, 1985. Two books that contain rhymes and very short stories for the flannel board. Each flannel board is ready to cut out and color.

Ring a Ring o' Roses: Stories, Games, and Finger Plays for Pre-School Children. Flint Public Library, 1971. The standard, must have book of basic fingerplays.

Schuman, Davida. "The Caregiver's Role in Emergent Literacy." *Children Today*, (September October 1990):20-21. Information on what adults can do to encourage literacy in young children.

Sierra, Judy. *The Flannel Board Storytelling Book.* H.W. Wilson, 1987. A collection of very tellable flannel board stories with patterns.

———. *Mother Goose's Play House.* Bob Kaminski Media Arts, 1994. Nursery rhymes and short stories are provided here with patterns for the flannel board and for puppets.

Silberg, Jackie. *Games to Play with Babies.* Gryphon House, 1993. Educational games that improve motor ability in children are explained in this book.

Story-Huffman, Ru. *Nursery Rhyme Time.* Alleyside Press, 1996. Twenty-eight programs created around some of the best-known nursery rhymes. Fingerplays and reproducibles for telling props.

Warren, Jean. *1 2 3 Puppets.* Warren House, 1989. This book has hundreds of ideas for simple puppets that can be used as giveaways or in your infant/toddler programs.

Wilmes, Liz and Dick. *2's Experience Felt Board Fun.* Building Blocks, 1994. Basic concepts are described in felt board stories, rhymes and songs. Patterns are included.

———. *2's Experience Fingerplays.* Building Blocks, 1994. Basic fingerplays are given with hand movements.

Sources to Purchase Props, Flannel Boards, and Other Materials

Creatively Yours Puppetry, 2906 West 64th Place, Tulsa, Oklahoma 74132. (800) 397-9652 Small people ($18.00) and animal ($12.00) puppets.

Highsmith Inc, W5527 Hwy 106, Fort Atkinson, Wisconsin 53538. (800) 558-2110. Hand puppets, puppet stages, flannel boards.

Nasco Learning Fun, 901 Janesville Avenue, Fort Atkinson, Wisconsin 53538. (800) 558-9595. Hand puppets, fingerplay mitts and characters, "mittboard," props, flannel boards.

The Storyteller, Melanie Chatterton, 11204 Jereme Trail, Frisco, Texas. 75034. (214) 335-8676. Flannel board pieces and flannel finger and hand puppets.

Title/Author Index

Subject Index to the Activities